Count Palmiro V

Grand Grimoire of

Bawdy Ballads
and
Limericks

The New Traveller's Companion Series, #92

COUNT PALMIRO VICARION'S BOOK OF BAWDY BALLADS
FIRST PUBLISHED 1955

COUNT PALMIRO VICARION'S BOOK OF LIMERICKS
FIRST PUBLISHED 1956

OLYMPIA PRESS.COM EDITION 2006

ISBN: 1-59654-321-3

THE OLYMPIA PRESS. A DVISION OF DISRUPTIVE PUBLISHING, INC.

Table of Contents

COUNT PALMIRO VICARION'S 4

BOOK OF BAWDY BALLADS 4

    I. THE WHEEL 7

    II. THE GREAT PLENIPOTENTIARY 8

    III. THE WHOLE WORLD OVER 12

    IV. THE PORTIONS OF THE FEMALE 14

    V. THE HOLE IN THE ELEPHANT'S BOTTOM 15

    VI. THE HEDGEHOG SONG 16

    VII. A CLEAN STORY 17

    VIII. POOR LITTLE ANGELINE 18

    IX. THE OLD APPLE TREE 20

    X. IN MOBILE 20

    XI. THE BASTARD KING OF ENGLAND 21

    XII. WALKING IN A MEADOW GREEN 23

    XIII. SERGEANT BOON 25

    XIV. ESKIMO NELL 26

    XV. AUBADE FOR THE SHITHOUSE 34

    XVI. THE HAPPY FAMILY 34

    XVII. THE YOUNGEST CHILD 35

XVIII. THE GOOD SHIP VENUS 36
XIX. THE TREE OF LIFE 37
XX. THE PURITAN MATHYAS 38
XXI. THE BALL OF KERRIMUIR..................... 39
XXII. THE MAIDEN'S LAMENT 42
XXIII. THE RAM OF DERBYSHIRE................. 43
XXIV. MONTE CARLO 43
XXV. THE VIRGIN STURGEON....................... 44
XXVI. BLINDED BY SHIT................................ 46
XXVII. MY LOVE IS FOR A BOLD MARINE . 47
XXVIII. SONIA SNELL 48
XXIX. LITTLE JIM... 49
XXX. MY JENNY WREN BRIDE 51
XXXI. THE CHORIC SONG OF THE MASTURBATORS 52
XXXII. THREE OLD WHORES FROM WINNIPEG.. 53
XXXIII. TALE ONE 54
XXXIV. TALE TWO 55
XXXV. TALE THREE.. 56
XXXVI. SHE WENT FOR A RIDE IN A

MORGAN 58

XXXVII. DOWN BY THE BARRACK GATE ... 59

XXXVIII. POOR BLIND NELL 60

XXXIX. THE STREET OF A THOUSAND ARSEHOLES 61

XXXX. I DON'T WANT TO JOIN THE ARMY 62

XXXXI. LITTLE SALLY 63

XXXXII. THE FARMER'S DOG 63

XXXXIII. I DREAMED MY LOVE 65

XXXXIV. THE COWPUNCHER'S WHORE 66

XXXXV. ARSEHOLES ARE CHEAP TODAY . 68

XXXXVI. OLLIE, OLLIE, OLLIE 68

XXXXVII. THE RAJAH OF ASTRAKAN 69

XXXXVIII. NIGHTFUCK 70

XXXXIX. THE HARLOT OF JERUSALEM 72

L. DIAMOND LILY 75

LI. THE KEYHOLE IN THE DOOR 75

LII. THE TRAVELIN' MAN 76

LIII. PLEASE DONT BURN OUR SHITHOUSE DOWN 78

LIV. TIM THE TINKER 78

LV. THE GREAT FARTING CONTEST 80

LVI. NO BALLS AT ALL 82

LVII. ALL THE NICE GIRLS 83

LVIII. THERE WAS A PRIEST 83

LIX. DEAD-EYE DICK AGAIN 84

LX. SALOME 84

LXI. THE BRICKLAYERS' UNION 85

LXII. ABDUL ABULBUL EMIR 86

LXIII. THE ONE-EYED RILEY 87

LXIV. LULU 88

LXV. FATHER'S GRAVE 89

COUNT PALMIRO VICARION'S 90

BOOK OF LIMERICKS 90

Index of First Lines 150

Count Palmiro Vicarion's Book of Bawdy Ballads

Acknowledgements: Many poets have helped me collect this book. I would like to thank in particular Madame Desiree Noblock of London and Mr. Gregory Kont of Bayswater. And I have by no means forgotten A.C., G.A.P., M.S., P.J., L.B., P.B., S.B., & J.C. of Paris and Zagreb.

Elated, no longer a child, dawn found me a literary man; I vowed Puffer would not have died in vain.

My parents were surprised at my docility when, after the funeral, they proposed I begin schooling in England. They little knew my plan of scholarship: Puffer had compiled but three volumes; I was persuaded greater wealth would be the reward of a more diligent scholar.

And how right I was. Hadn't he overlooked:

'Don't look at me that way, barman I ain't gonna shit on the floor'?

He had indeed, and many others. He was not a man to track down those who "know them all by heart" or even those who have "bits of songs". No, he was a dilettante, I came to see that. But even with greatest effort the scholar is always encountering the person who knows but two lines (often glorious) and just a snatch of the melody. He will usually direct you to someone else who knows perhaps the same two lines or just one more... Ah, it is not easy. And while great songs exist which I have not compiled here, it is simply that I have been unable to track down the complete version — of, to take an example. 'The Ballad of Piss-Pot-Pete'. And then there was that girl from Miss Brice's School — all golden she was and with a voice like a morning lark's — but for the life of me I can remember no more of her song than its lilting refrain:

'Oh how did Edith ever
Get so shitty round the titty?'

You either write them down then and there or they are

gone. It is quite like the limerick except that you may be left with no more than a bit of a tune.

Luckily, I was found physically fit for my country's wars (and it was with some apprehension I limped into enlistment headquarters, looking askance to conceal my missing eye) for without those enriching experiences my collection would be paltry indeed. Oh, it is in war the bawdy ballad thrives: up to the waist in urine or blood or even rain, men begin to sing, and richly. I must say I have never well understood why it is those who order and control such fine wars are so prudish about the cultural harvest that are reaped from a really sopping trench or freezing billet. But no matter. I have prudently, I believe, never allowed such reflections to distract me from my scholarly dedication. I felt I owed that to Puffer.

Thanks to a courageous and cultivated publisher, the same who saw the Limerick for the treasure it is, I can here present the cream of my years of research. I have included some music and have simply named familiar tunes appropriate to other ballads. For the rest, many tunes exist, but the common 4/4 ballad rhythm will usually do. And besides, I have come to feel that the dirty song tune is almost instinctive. Even the song itself: rarely is a ballad sung the same way twice, nor, I strongly feel, should it be. If a person has something to add, let him. And if someone tells you your version of 'Don't Piss on the Fire Grandma, Father is Warming his Ball's' is incorrect, be sure it is the same pedant who will suggest your joke would be funnier if it ended another way. Kick him, I say.

Vicarion. 1956. Alma Atta.

I. THE WHEEL

To the tune of the hymn, "Oh Master, Let me Walk With Thee"

A sailor told me 'ere he died,
And I do not think the bastard lied,
That his wife's cunt was made so wide,
She never could be satisfied.
So he built a prick of steel,
Fastened it to a bloody great wheel,
Nine feet long and stuffed with cream,
And the whole fucking issue was driven by steam.
Round and round went the fucking great wheel,
In and out went the prick of steel;
Till at last the lady cried— "Enough!
Enough! I'm satisfied!"
But this was a case of the biter bit,
There was no way of stopping it;
She was split from arse to tit,
And the whole fucking issue was covered in—
   Sweet violets,
      Sweeter than all the roses.
   Covered all over from arse to tit,
      Covered all over with—
   Sweet violets...

II. THE GREAT PLENIPOTENTIARY

The Bey of Algiers when afraid for his ears,
    A messenger sent to our court,
Sir; As he knew in our State that the women have weight,
    He chose one well hung for good sport, Sir;
He searched the Divan till he found out a man,
    Whose bollocks were heavy and hairy,
And he lately came o'er from the Barbary Shore,
    As the Great Plenipotentiary.
When to England he came with his prick all aflame,
    And showed to his hostess on landing,
Whence spread its renown to all parts of the town,
    As a pintle past all understanding.
So much there was said of its snout and its head,
    They called it the great Janissary,
Not a Lady could sleep till she got a shy peep
    At the Great Plenipotentiary.
As he rode in his coach how the whores did approach,
    And they stared as if stretched on a tenter;
He drew every eye of the dames that passed by,
    Like the wonderful sun to its centre.
As he passed through the town not a window was down,
    And the maids hurried out just to see;
And the children cried, "Look—at the man with the cock,
    That's the Great Plenipotentiary."
When he came to the Court, O what giggle and sport!
    Such squinting and squeezing to view him!
What envy and spleen in the women were seen,
    Of the happy and pleased that got to him.
They vowed in their hearts, if men of such parts
    Were found in the coast of Barbary

'Twas a shame not to bring a whole guard for 'the King,
    Like the Great Plenipotentiary.
The dames of intrigue formed their cunts in a league,
    To take him in turn like good folk, Sirs;
The young Misses' plan was to catch as catch can,
    And all were resolved on a stroke, Sirs!
The cards to invite flew by thousands each night,
    With bribes to his old Secretary,
And the famous Eclipse was not let for more leaps,
    Than the Great Plenipotentiary.
When his name was announced how the women all bounced,
    And the blood hurried up to their faces;
He made them all itch from the nave to the breech,
    And their bubbies burst out of their laces.
There was such damned work to be fucked by the Turk,
    That nothing their passion could vary;
The whole Nation fell sick for the Tripoli prick
    Of the Great Plenipotentiary.
The Duchess who's Duke made her ready to puke
    With fumbling and friggin' all night, Sir,
Being first with the prize was so pleased by its size,
    That she begged to examine its plight, Sir!
"Good God,", cried Her Grace, "its head's like a mace!
    'Tis as big as a Corsican Fairy!
I'll make up—please the pigs—for dry-bobs and frigs,
    With the Great Plenipotentiary."
And now to be bored by this Ottoman Lord,
    Came a virgin far gone in the wane, Sir;
She resolved for to try, though her cunt was so dry,
    That she knew it must split like a cane, Sir!
True it was as she spoke—it gave way at each stroke,
    But O what a terrible quandary,
With one mighty thrust her old piss-bladder bust

    On the Great Plenipotentiary.
The next to be tried was an Alderman's bride,
    With a cunt that would swallow a turtle,
Who had horned the dull brows of her worshipful spouse,
    Till they sprouted like Venus's myrtle.
Through thick and through thin, bowel deep he dashed in,
    Till her quim frothed like cream in a dairy,
And expressed by loud farts she was strained in all parts
    By the Great Plenipotentiary.
The next to be kissed by the Plenipo's lift
    Was a delicate maiden of honour,
She screamed at the sight of his prick in a fright,
    Though she had the whole place upon her:
"Cunt Jesus," she said, "what a prick for a maid,
    Do pray come and look at it Mary."
Then she cried with a grunt, "O he's ruined my cunt
    With his Great Plenipotentiary!"
Two sisters next came—Peg and Mary by name,
    Two ladies of very high breeding,
Resolved one should try whilst the other stood by
    To assist in the bloody proceeding:
Peg swore by her God that the Musselman's nob,
    Was thick as the buttocks of Mary,
"But I'll have one drive if I'm ripped up alive
    By the Great Plenipotentiary."
All twats were bewitched and just longed to be stitched,
    Even fairies would languish and linger,
And the boarding school Miss as she sat down to piss
    Drew a Turk on the floor with her finger.
By fancy so struck they clubbed round for a fuck,
    And bought a huge candle and hairy,
And the teachers from France they fuck'd *a distance,*

With the Great Plenipotentiary.
Each sluice cunted bawd who was knocked all abroad,
 Till her premises gaped like a grave, Sir,
Hoped her luck was on, so she'd feel the Turk's dong,
 As all others were lost in her cave, Sir.
The nymphs of the stage his fine parts did engage,
 Made him free of the grand feminary,
And gentle Signors opened all their black doors
 To the Great Plenipotentiary.
Of love's sweet reward measured out by the yard,
 The Turk was most blest of mankind, Sir,
For his powerful dart went home to the heart.
 Whether stuck in before or behind, Sir.
But no pencil can draw this long donged Pawshaw,
 Than each cunt loving contemporary.
But as pricks of the game let's drink health to the name
 Of the Great Plenipotentiary!

III. THE WHOLE WORLD OVER

She was poor but she was honest
   Victim of a rich man's whim,
First he fucked her then he left her
   And she had a child by him.
It's the same the whole world over,
   It's the poor wot gets the blame,
It's the rich wot gets the pleasure,
   'Ain't it all a bleedin' shame?
Standing on the bridge at midnight,
   Throwing snowballs at the moon,
She said, "George I've never 'ad it."
   But she spoke too fuckin' soon.
It's &c
Then she came to London city,
   To recover her fair name,
But another bastard fucked her,
   Now she's on the streets again.
It's &c
Standing on the bridge at midnight,
   Cracking walnuts with her crutch,
She said, "Jack I've never 'ad it."
   He said, "No? Not fuckin' much!"
It's &c
See the little country cottage,
   Where her simple parents live,
Though they drink the fizz she sends 'em,
   On her achin' quim they live.
It's &c
Now she stands in Piccadilly,
   Pickin' blackheads from her quim,
She is now completely ruined,
   And it's all because of him.

It's &c
She got pox and 'orrid chankers,
   From the wolves that plumbed her gut,
So she went down to the river,
   For to give her whorin' up.
It's &c
As they pulled her from the water,
   Water from her clothes they rung,
And they thought that she had had it,
   But the corpse got up and sung.
It's &c
See him seated in his Bentley,
   Coming homeward from the hunt,
He got riches from his marriage,
   She got corns upon her cunt.
It's &c
See him in the House of Commons,
   Passing laws for all mankind,
While she walks the streets of London,
   Selling chunks of her behind.
It's &c

IV. THE PORTIONS OF THE FEMALE
The portions of a woman that appeal to man's depravity,
   Are fashioned with considerable care,
And what at first appears to be a simple little cavity,
   Is really an elaborate affair.
Now surgeons who have studied these feminine phenomena,
   By numerous experiments on Dames
Have taken all the items of the gentle sex's abdomina,
   And given them delightful Latin names.
There's the Vulva, the Vagina and the good old Peronina,
   And the Hymen that is sometimes found in brides,
There's a lot of little things—you'd love 'em could you see
   The Clitoris and God knows what besides.
['em
What a pity it is then, when we common people chatter
   Of those mysteries to which I have referred,
We use for such a delicate and complicated matter,
   Such a very short and unattractive little word.
The erudite authorities who study the geography
   Of that obscure but entertaining land,
Are able to indulge a taste for intricate topography,
   And view the tasty details close at hand.
But ordinary people though aware of their existence,
   And complexities beneath the public *know*
Are normally contented to view them at a distance,
   And treat them roughly speaking as a show.
And therefore when we laymen probe the secrets of virginity,
   We exercise a simple sense of touch,
We don't cloud the issue with meticulous Latinity,
   But call the whole concern a simple CUNT.

    For men have made this useful and intelligent commodity,
    The topic of innumerable jibes,
    And though the name they call it by, is something of an oddity,
    It seems to fit the subject they describe.

V. THE HOLE IN THE ELEPHANT'S BOTTOM

My ambition's to go on the stage;
From this you can see that I've got 'em.
In pantomime I'm all the rage,
I'm the hole in the elephant's bottom.
Oh! The girls all think that I'm it,
As they sit in the stalls I can spot 'em,
And I wink at the girls in the pit
Through the hole in the elephant's bottom.
One night we performed in a farce
And they stuffed up the bottom with cotton,
But it split and I showed my bare arse
Through the hole in the elephant's bottom.
There are pockets inside in the cloth
For two bottles of Bass, if you've got 'em.
But they hiss and they boo when I blow out the froth
Through the hole in the elephant's bottom.
Now my part hasn't got any words
But there's nothing that can't be forgotten,
I spent all my time pushing property turds
Through the hole in the elephant's bottom.
Some may think that this story is good
And some may believe that it's rotten,
But those that don't like it can stuff it right up
The hole in the elephant's bottom.

Should the Japanese make an attack,
Then hundreds of bombs—they will drop 'em,
But we'll keep 'em at bay with an Oerliken gun
Through the hole in the elephant's bottom.

VI. THE HEDGEHOG SONG
Recent extensive researches
   By Darwin, Huxley and Ball,
Have conclusively proved that the hedgehog
   Has never been buggered at all.
Sing Torrel-i-orrel-i-orrel
   Sing Torrel-i-orrel-i-aye,.
Sing Torrel-i-orrel-i-orrel
   Sing Torrel-i-orrel-i-aye.
Further experimentations
   Have incontrovertibly shown
That comparative safety at Harvard
   Is enjoyed by the hedgehog alone.
Sing Torrel &c.
In the process of syphilisation
   From anthropoid ape down to man,
The palm is awarded to Harvard
   For buggering whatever it can.
Sing Torrd &c.
This rough little, tough little bastard
   Has got prickles all over his arse,
But the students of Yale have now mastered,
   A method of slipping it past.
Sing Torrel &c.
Now why don't they do down at Harvard
   What they finally learnt up at Yale
And get over this difficult problem
   By shaving the hairs off its tail.

VII. A CLEAN STORY

There was an old sailor who sat on a rock
Waving his fists and abusing his
Neighbouring farmer watching his ricks,
Teaching his children to play with their
Kites and marbles as in days of yore
When along came a woman who looked like a
Decent young lady and walked like a duck.
She said she was learning a new way to
Bring up her children and teach them to knit.
While the boys in the farmyard were shovelling
The contents of the pigsty, the muck and the mire,
The squire of the Manor was pulling his
Horse from its stable to go to the hum,
His wife in her boudoir was powdering her
Nose and arranging her vanity box
And taking precautions to ward off the
Gout and rheumatics which made her feel stiff,
For well did she remember her last dose of
What did you think I was going to say?
No, you rude bugger, that's all for today.

VIII. POOR LITTLE ANGELINE
She was sweet sixteen, Little Angeline,
Always playing on the village green,
Never had a thrill, was a virgin still,
    Poor Little Angeline.
Now the local Squire got a low desire,
The biggest bastard'in the whole damn Shire,
And he set his heart on the vital part
    Of Poor Little Angeline.
Carne the village fair, and the Squire was there,
Masturbating in the village square,
When he chanced to see the comely knee
    Of Poor Little Angeline.
As she raised her skirt to avoid the dirt,
Skipping o'er the puddles of the Squire's last squirt.
As the thigh he saw, how his nob grew raw,
    Of Poor Little Angeline.
As he raised his cap, he said "Miss, your cat
Has been run over and is squashed quite flat.
My car's in the square, so I'll take you there,
    My Poor Little Angeline."
They had not gone far when he stopped the car,
And dragged the maiden to the Public Bar,
With a load of gin she would fear no sin,
    Poor Little Angeline.
Now the dirty old turd should have got the bird,
Instead she followed him without a word,
As she drove away you could hear them say
    "Poor Little Angeline."
He had oiled her well, got her in a dell,
And there decided that he'd give her hell,
So he tried his luck with a dog-like fuck,
    At Poor Little Angeline.
Angeline cried "Rape," as he raised her cape,

Unhappy darlin' there was no escape,
'Twas time someone came for to save the name
    Of Poor Little Angeline.
Now it can be told that the blacksmith bold,
Had loved Little Angeline from time untold,
He was handsome, true, and virile too
    Poor Little Angeline.
But sad to say on that self-same day,
The blacksmith had been put in gaol to stay,
For he soaked his pants at the village dance
    With Poor Little Angeline.
Now the bars of the cell overlooked the dell,
Where the Squire was trying to give the maiden hell,
As they reached the grass, he saw the arse
    Of his Poor Little Angeline.
So he gave a start and let out a fart,
Strong enough to blow the bars apart,
And he ran like shit, 'cause the Squire might split
    Poor Little Angeline.
When he reached the spot and he saw what's what,
He tied the villain's penis in a grannie knot,
And he kicked his guts, bruised the poor sod's nuts,
    Poor Little Angeline.
"Blacksmith I love you—oh indeed I do.
I can see by your trousers that you love me too!
As I am undressed—come and try your best
    For Poor Little Angeline."

IX. THE OLD APPLE TREE
In the shade of the old apple tree,
   A pair of fine legs I did see,
With some hairs at the top,
   And a little red spot,
It looked like a cherry to me.
I pulled out my pride of New York.
   It filled it just like a cork;
I said, "Darlin' don't scream,
   While I dish out the cream
In the shade of the old apple tree."
And as we both lay on the grass,
   With my two hands round her fat arse
She said "If you'll be true,
   You can have a suck too!"
In the shade of the old apple tree."

X. IN MOBILE
Air: She'll Be Coming Round The Mountain
Oh the shitehawks they fly high in Mobile,
Oh the shite hawks they fly high in Mobile,
   Oh the shite hawks they fly high
   And they shit right in your eye,
It's a good things cows can't fly in Mobile.
Oh the old brown cow is dead in Mobile,
   But the children must be fed
So we'll milk the bull instead in Mobile.
There's a lady they call Susan in Mobile,
   And her cunt she's always usin'
She's got the best infusion in Mobile.
There's a shortage of good whores in Mobile,
   So we'll fuck the shithouse doors,
And there's knotholes in the floor in Mobile.

Oh I knew a parson's daughter in Mobile
    Sought her, caught her, fucked her, taught her,
Now I cannot pass my water in Mobile.
Among the upper classes in Mobile
    When they finished with their glasses
They just stuff them up their arses in Mobile.
There's no paper in the bogs in Mobile,.
There's no paper in the bogs in Mobile,
    There's no paper in the bogs
    So we'll shit until it clogs
Then we'll saw it off in logs in Mobile.
Note: only the first and last stanzas are given in the form best for singing.

XI. THE BASTARD KING OF ENGLAND

The minstrels sing of a bastard King
    Of a thousand years ago,
Who ruled this land with an iron hand
    Though his mind was mean and low.
He was very fond of hunting,
    And roving the Royal wood,
He was also fond of apple-jack,
    And pulling the Royal pud.
He was forty, fat, and full o' fleas,
    The Royal nob hung next his knees
Twelve inches long and a two inch span,
    As King he made a dirty old man.
Now the Queen of Spain was an amorous dame,
    And a sprightly wench was she;
She longed to fool with the Royal tool
    Of the King across the sea.
So she sent a secret message
    By a lean ambassador,

To ask the King if he would spend
    A month in bed with her.
Now Philip of France when he heard this chance,
    Within his Royal court, He swore
"By God, she loves his nob.
    Because my tool is short!" o
So he sent the rotten Due d'Alsace
    To give the Queen a dose of clap,
To ruin the length and burn the sap
    Of the Bastard King of England.
When news of this foul deed was heard,
    Within fair London's walls,
The King he swore by the Royal Whore
    He'd have King Philip's balls.
And he issued a proclamation
    That a tuft of the Queen's cunt hair
He'd give to the sod who brought him the rod,
    And the nuts of Philip the fair.
The brave young Duke of Buckingham
    Went instantly to France
And lay that night with the Royal catamite
    And when he downed his pants,
He fastened a thong to Fair Philip's dong
    Jumped on horse and galloped along,
Over the cliffs and under the seas
    And brought them both to the Bastard's knees.
Now all the whores in silken drawers,
    Sat on the castle walls,
When the Duke sang "King, I got his thing!"
    They merely answered "Balls".
But the King threw up his breakfast,
    And grovelled on the floor,
For in the ride the French King's pride
    Had stretched a yard or more.

And Philip alone usurped his throne,
    His sceptre was his Royal bone,
He fucked each member of the Realm
    And the Bastard King went down to hell.

XII. WALKING IN A MEADOW GREEN
Walking in a meadow green,
    Fair flowers for to gather,
Where primrose ranks did stand on banks
    To welcome comers thither,
I heard a voice which made a noise,
    And caused me to attend it,
I heard a lass say to a lad,
    "Once more, and none can mend it."
They lay so close together,
    They made me much to wonder,
I knew not which was whether,
    Until I saw her under.
Then off he carne and blushed for shame,
    So soon that he had ended;
Yet still she lies, and to him cries,
    "Once more, and none can mend it!"
His looks were dull and very sad,
    His courage she had tamed;
She bade him play the lusty lad
    Or quit and be ashamed.
"So stiffly thrust, and hit me just,
    Fear not but freely spend it,
Come, play about, now in—now out,
    "Once more, and none can mend it!"
At last he thought to enter her,
    Thinking the horn was on him;
But when he came to enter her,

The point turned back upon him.
She said, "O stay! Go not away,
   Although the point be bended!
But plunge again, and hit the vein!
   "Once more, and none can mend it!"
Then in her arms she did him fold,
   And oftentimes she kissed him,
Yet still his courage was but cold
   For all the good she wished him;
With her white hand she made it stand
   So stiff she could not bend it,
And then anon she cried, "Come on
   "Once more, and none can mend it!"
"Adieu, adieu, sweetheart," said he,
   "For in faith I must be gone."
"Nay, then you do me wrong," quoth she,
   "To leave me thus alone."
Away he went when all was spent,
   And she was most offended;
Like a Trojan True she made a vow,
   She'd soon have one to mend it!

XIII. SERGEANT BOON
Hear us sing of Sergeant Boon,
Who used to sleep in the afternoon,
   So tired was he,
   So tired was he.
Down in the woods he used to go,
To *doze* away an hour or so.
   Down came a bee,
   Busy little bumble-bee.
   Bsz, bzz, bzz, bzs,
   Busy bee, busy bee.
"Get away you bumble bee,
   I ain't no rose;
I ain't no syphilitic bastard,
   Get off my fuckin' nose.
Get off my nasal organ,
   Don't you come near,
If you wanta bit o' fanny
   You can fuck my Granny,
But you'll get no arsehole here."
   Arsehole rules the Navy,
   Arsehole rules the sea:
   If you wanta bit o' bum,
   You can fuck my chum,
   But you'll get no arse from me!

XIV. ESKIMO NELL

When a man grows old and his balls grow cold an the
 [end of his nob turns blue,
When it's bent in the middle like a one-string fiddle, he can
 [tell a yarn or two.
So find me a seat and stand me a drink and a tale to you
 [I'll tell,
Of Dead-Eye Dick and Mexico Pete and the gentle Eskimo
 [Nell.
Now when Dead-Eye Dick and Mexico Pete go forth in
 [search of fun,
It's usually Dick who wields the prick and Mexico Pete
 [the gun.
And when Dead-Eye Dick and Mexico Pete are sore
 [depressed and mad,
'Tis a cunt that generally bears the brunt—so the shootin'
 ['ain't too bad.
Now Dead-Eye Dick and Mexico Pete had been hunting
 [in Dead Man's Creek,
And they'd had no luck in the way of a fuck for nigh on
 [half a week.
Just a moose or two or a caribou and a bison-cow or so,
And for Dead-Eye Dick with his kingly prick this fucking
 [was mighty slow.
So do or dare this horny pair set out for the Rio Grande,
Dead-Eye Dick with his muscular prick and Pete with
 [his gun in hand
They blazed a randy trail and no man in their path
 [withstood,
And many a bride who was hubby's pride knew

pregnant

[widowhood.
They made the strand of the Rio Grande at the height of
[a blazing noon,
And to slake their thirst and fo' their worst they sought
[Black Mike's saloon.
As the swing doors opened wide, both prick and gun
[flashed free,
"Accordin' to sex, you bleedin' wrecks, you drinks or fucks

[with me!"
Now they'd heard of the prick called Dead-Eye Dick from
[the Horn to Panama,
And with nothing worse than a muttered curse those
[cowhands sought the bar.
The women too knew his playful ways down on the Rio
[Grande,
And forty whores took down their drawers at Dead-Eye

[Dick's command.
They saw the fingers of Mexico Pete twitch on the trigger
[grip.
'Twas death to wait—at a fearful rate those whores began

[to strip.
Now Dead-Eye Dick was breathing quick with lecherous
[snorts and grunts,
As forty arses were bared to view to say nothing of forty

Now forty arses and forty cunts you'll see if you use your [wits,
And rattle a bit at arithmetic—that's likewise eighty tits.

And eighty tits is a gladsome sight for a man with a raging [stand,
They may be rare in Berkeley Square, but not on the Rio [Grande.
Our Dead-Eye Dick he fucks 'em quick, so he backed and [took a run,
He made a dart at the nearest tart and scored a bull in one.

He bore her to the sandy floor and fucked her deep and fine,
And though she grinned it put the wind up the other [thirty-nine.
Our Dead-Eye Dick he fucks 'em quick, and flinging the [first aside,
He was making a gin at the second quim when the swing [doors opened wide.
And into that hall of sin and vice—into that harlot's hell
Strode a gentle maid who was unafraid, and her name [was Eskimo Nell.
Our Dead-Eye Dick who fucks 'em quick was well in [No. 22,
When Eskimo Nell lets out a yell and says to him, "Hey—

[you."
The hefty lout he turned about, both nob and face were red,
With a single flick of his mighty prick the tart flew o'er
[his head.
But Eskimo Nell she stood it well and looked him in the
[eyes,
With the utmost scorn she glimpsed the horn that rose from

[his hairy thighs.
She blew a puff from her cigarette onto his steaming nob,
So utterly beat was Mexico Pete he forgot to do his job.
It was Eskimo Nell who broke the spell in accents calm
[and cool,
"You cunt-struck shrimp of a Yankee pimp, do you call

[that thing a tool?"
"If this here town can't take that down," she sneered to
[the cowering whores—
"There's one little cunt that can do the stunt—it's Eskimo
[Nell's not yours."
She shed her garments one by one with an air of conscious
[pride,
Till at last she stood in her womanhood, and they saw the

[great divide.
She laid right down on the table top where someone had
[left a glass,

With a twitch of her tits she crushed it to bits between the

[cheeks of her arse!
She bent her knees with supple ease and opened her legs [apart;
With a final nod to the randy sod she gave him the cue

[to start.
But Dead-Eye Dick with his King of a prick prepared to [take his time,
For a girl like this was a fucking bliss—so he staged a

[pantomime.
He winked his arsehole in and out, and made his balls [innate,
Until they looked like granite knobs on top of a garden gate.

He rubbed his foreskin up and down—his nob increased [in size,
His mighty prick grew twice as thick and almost reached

[his eyes.
He polished the rod with Rum and gob to make it steaming
[hot,
And to finish the job he sprinkled the nob with a cayenne

[pepper pot.
He didn't back to take a run, nor yet a flying leap;
But bent right down and came longside with a steady [forward creep.

Then he took a sight as a gunman might along his mighty
[tool,
And shoved his lust with a dexterous thrust—firm, calculat-

[ing and cool.
Have you seen the massive pistons on the giant C.P.R.?
With a punishing force of a thousand horses—you know
[what pistons are.
Or you think you do, but you've yet to learn the awe-
[inspiring trick,
Of the work that's done on a non-stop run by a man like
[Dead-Eye Dick.
But Eskimo Nell was an Infidel—she equalled a whole
[harem,
With the strength of ten in her abdomen and her rock of

[ages beam.
Amidships she could stand the rush like, the flush of a
[water closet,
So she grasped his cock like a Chatwood lock on the

[National Safe Deposit.
She lay for a while with a subtle smile while the grip of
[her cunt grew keener,
Then giving a sigh she sucked him dry with the ease of a
[vacuum cleaner.
She performed this feat in a way so neat as to set at
[complete defiance
The primary cause and the basic laws that govern sexual
[science.
She calmly rode through the phallic code which for years

[had stood the test,
And the ancient laws of the Classic school in a moment [or two went west.
And now my friend we draw to the end of this copulating
[epic,
The effect on Dick was sudden and quick and akin to an

[anaesthetic.
He slipped to the floor and he knew no more—his passions
[extinct and dead—
He didn't shout as his tool came out; it was stripped down
[to a thread.
Mexico Pete, he sprang to his feet, to avenge his pal's
[affront,
With a fearful jolt he drew his Colt and rammed it up her

[cunt.
He shoved it up to the trigger grip and fired three times
[three,
But to his surprise she rolled her eyes and smiled in ecstasy.

She leaped to her feet with a smile so sweet, "Bully," she
[said, "for you,
Though I might have guessed it's about the best you phoney
[lechers do.
When next your friend and you intend to sally forth for
[fun,

Buy Dead-Eye Dick a sugar stick, and get yourself a bun.

I'm going back to the frozen North, to the land where [spunk is Spunk,
Not a trickling stream of lukewarm cream—but a solid [frozen chunk.
Back to the land where they understand what it means to [fornicate,
Where even the dead sleep two in a bed and the infants

[copulate.
Back to the land of the mighty stand, where the nights are
[six months long,
Where the polar bear whanks off in his lair—that's where
[they'll sing this song."
They'll tell this tale on the Artie trail where the nights are
[sixty below,
Where it's so damn cold, french letters are sold wrapped in

[a ball of snow.
In the valley of death with baited breath it's there we sing
[it too,
Where the skeletons rattle in sexual battle, and the

[mouldering corpses screw!

XV. AUBADE FOR THE SHITHOUSE
Come away my love with me
To the public lavatory.

There is an expert there who can,
Encircle thrice the glittering pan.
He, happy youth, has no idea
What suffers from diarrhoea
Expelling clouds of noisome vapours
Spend annually on toilet papers.
But tranquilly pursues his art,
Or rocks the building with a fart.
O come away my love with me,
To the public lavatory.

XVI. THE HAPPY FAMILY

Air: Deutschland Uber Alles
Life presents a doleful picture,
All around is murk and gloom:
Father has an anal stricture,
Mother has a fallen womb.
In a corner sits Jemina,
Never laughs and rarely smiles;
What a dismal occupation,
Cracking ice for Father's piles.
Cousin James has been deported,
For a homosexual crime:
While the housemaid has aborted,
For the twenty-second time.
Bill the baby's no exception,
For he's always having fits;
Every time he laughs he vomits,
Every time he farts—he shits.
Cousin Jo has won the Hackney
Masturbation marathon,
But has died of self-expression
Since he buggered Uncle Tom.

Bert the postman called this morning,
Stuck his penis through—the door,
We could not, despite endearment,
Get it out till half past four.
In a small brown paper parcel,
Wrapped in a mysterious way,
Is an imitation arsehole
Granpaw uses twice a day.
From the boghouse hear him yelling,
No one helps the ancient lout,
For the plug is in his arsehole,
And he cannot get it out.

XVII. THE YOUNGEST CHILD
No air known
She lay nude between the sheets
    And I beside her lay;
And she was soft and round and chubby,
    Under my hand uprose her bubby.
My hand beneath her waist did stroke,
    Her tip-tops itched and tingled,
I clambered up, began to poke,
    And our juices intermingled.
"Pull out! Pull out!" the fair one cried,
    "Before I swell with trouble."
I did. And on her snow white breast
    My come did froth and bubble.
I gazed into her frightened eyes
    And with a leery curse
"This is the youngest child," I said,
    "That you will ever nurse."
She picked it up with one fair hand,
    And with a shocked "Oh La!"

She threw the load into my face,
   Saying, "Child, go kiss your Pa!"

XVIII. THE GOOD SHIP VENUS
'Twas on the good ship Venus,
By Christ you should have seen us;
The figure-head was a whore in bed,
And the mast was a rampant penis.
The Captain of this lugger
He was a filthy bugger,
Declared unfit to shovel shit
From one ship to another.
The cabin-boy called Dripper,
Was a foul-mouthed little nipper,
Who stuffed his arse with broken glass
To circumcise the Skipper.
The first mate's name was Morgan,
A veritable Gorgon;
Each night at eight, he'd play till late
Upon his extra-sexual organ.
The boatswain was named Andy—
A Portsmouth man and randy—
His whopping cock broke chunks of rock,
To cool the Skipper's brandy.
His wife was baptised Charlotte
Who was born and bred a harlot.
At night her cunt was lily-white,
In the morning it was scarlet.
The Captain's daughter Mabel
Though young was fresh and able
To suck and shake and fornicate
Upon the chart-room table.
His other little daughter

Got shoved into the water,
Her plaintive squeals announced that eels
Had found her sexual quarter.
The ship's dog was called Rover,
We turned the poor thing over,
And ground and ground that faithful hound,
From Teneriffe to Dover.
Though skilful navigation
We reached our China station.
We sunk a junk on a sea of spunk
Through mutual masturbation.

XIX. THE TREE OF LIFE
Come prick up your ears, and attend Sirs, awhile;
I'll sing ye a song that'll cause ye to smile;
'Tis a faithful description of the tree of life,
So pleasing to ev'ry maid, widow and wife.
This tree it a succulent plant I declare,
Consisting of only one straight stem, I swear,
Its top sometimes looks like a cherry in May,
At other times more like a filbert they say.
This tree universal all countries produce,
But till eighteen years growth 'tis not much fit for use;
Then nine or ten inches—it seldom grows higher,
And that's sure as much as the heart can desire.
Its juice taken inward's a cure for the spleen,
And removes in an instant the sickness called *Green;*
Tho' sometimes it causes large tumors below,
They disperse of themselves in nine months or so.
It cures all dissentions 'twixt husband and wife,
And makes her look pleasant through each stage of life,
By right application it never can fail,
But then it is always put in through the tail.

Ye Ladies that long for a sight of this tree,
Take this invitation—come hither to me,
I have it just now at the height of perfection,
Adjusted for handling and fit for injection!

XX. THE PURITAN MATHYAS
There was a puritanical lad
And he was called Mathyas,
Who wished to go to Amsterdam
To speak with Ananyas.
He had not gone past half a mile,
But he met a holy sister,
He laid his bible under her cunt,
And merrily he kissed her.
"Alas! what would the wicked say?"
Said she, "if they had seen it!
My buttocks need some bolstering,
So put the Gospels in it!"
"But peace sweetheart, for ere we part—
I speak from pure devotion—
By aye or nay I'll not away,
Until you taste my motions."
They made full stride with many a heave,
Until they both were tired,
"Alas," said she, "you 'fuck with glee,
And my petticoats are all mired.
If we professors of the Lamb
To the English congregation,
Either at Leyden or Amsterdam,
It would disgrace the nation."
"But since it is, that part we must.
Though I am much unwilling,
Good brother have another thrust,

And take from me this shilling,
To pay your way for many a day
And feed your prick with filling."
Then down she laid, the holy maid,
And drained him at a sitting.

XXI. THE BALL OF KERRIMUIR
'Twas at the gatherin' of the Clans,
    And all the Scots were there,
'A feelin' up the lassies
    Among the pubic hair.
Singin' balls to your partner
    Arse against the wall,
If you can't get fucked this Saturday night,
    You'll never get fucked at all.
There was fucking in the haystacks,
    Fucking in the ricks,
You couldn't hear the music,
    For the swishin' of the pricks.
Singin' &c
The Undertaker he was there,
    Dressed in a long black shroud,
Swingin' from a chandelier,
    And pissin' on the crowd.
Singin' &c
The village cripple he was there,
    But didn't shag too much,
His old John Thomas had fallen off
    So he fucked 'em with his crutch.
Singin' &c
The local sweepy he was there,
    A really filthy brute,
And every time he farted,

He covered 'em all with soot.
Singin' &c
The village idiot he was there,
    Up to his favourite trick,
Bouncin' on his testicles,
    And whistlin' through his prick.
Singin' &c
The district nurse was there as well,
    She had us all in fits,
Jumping off the mantlepiece,
    And landin' on her tits.
Singin' &c
The village copper he was there,
    He had a mighty tool,
He pulled his foreskin o'er his head,
    And yodeled through the hole.
Singin' &c
The country postman he was there,
    He had a dose of pox,
As he couldn't fuck the lassies,
    He stuffed the letter box.
Singin' &c
The old fishmonger he was there,
    A dirty stinkin' sod,
He never got a stand that night,
    So he fucked 'em with a cod.
Singin' &c
The local Vicar he was there,
    His collar back to front,
He said "My girls thy sins are blest."
    And shoved it up their cunts.
Singin' &c
There was buggery in the parlour,
    Sodomy on the stairs,

You couldn't see the dancin' floor,
   For the mass of pubic hairs.
Singin' &c
There was wee Dr. Jameson,
   The one that fought the Boers,
He leaped up on the table,
   And shouted for the whores.
Singin' &c
Jock the blacksmith he was there,
   He couldn't play the game,
He fucked a lassie seven times
   And wouldn't see her hame.
Singin' &c
The village elders they were there,
   And they were shocked to see,
Four and twenty maidenheads
   A hangin' from a tree.
Singin' &c
The old schoolmaster he was there,
   He fucked by rule of thumb;
By logarithms he worked out
   The time that he would come.
Singin' &c
Four and twenty virgins,
   Came down from Cuiremore,
Only two got back again,
   And they were double bore.
Singin' &c
In the morning early,
   The farmer nearly shat,
For twenty acres of his corn,
   Were fairly ' fuckin' flat.
Singin' &c
And when the ball was over,

The maidens all confessed,
Although they liked the music
The fucking was the best.
Singin' &c

XXII. THE MAIDEN'S LAMENT
Once I was a servant girl who worked in Drury Lane,
The Master he was kind to me, the mistress was the same.
Early one evening, a sailor came to tea,
And that was the beginning of all my misery,
He asked me for a candle to light his way to bed,
He asked me for a pillow to rest his weary head.
And I like a silly girl not meaning any harm,
Jumped in beside him to keep the sailor warm.
Early next morning the sailor he awoke,
And he took from his pocket a rusty ten-bob note.
"Take this my darlin' for the damage I have done,
If it be a daughter or if it be a son.
If it be a daughter nurse her on your knee.
If it be a son chase the bastard off to sea.
With bell bottom trousers and a suit of Navy blue,
Let him climb the rigging the way I climbed up you!"
Now all of you young servant girls listen to my plea,
Never let a sailor one inch above your knee.

XXIII. THE RAM OF DERBYSHIRE
There was a ram of Derbyshire
   That had two horns of brass,
The one grew out of its head, sir,
   The other grew out of its arse.

If you don't believe me
　　Or if you think I lie,
So ask the girls of Derbyshire,
　　They'll tell you the same as I.
When the ram was young, sir,
　　It had a nasty trick
Of jumping over a five-barred gate
　　And landing on its prick.
If you don't believe &c.
When the ram was old, sir,
　　They put it in a truck
And all the girls of Derbyshire
　　Came out to have a fuck.
If you don't believe &c.
When the ram was dead, sir,
　　They buried it in St. Paul's,
It took twelve men and a donkey-cart
　　To carry away its balls.
If you don't believe &c.

XXIV. MONTE CARLO

As she walked along the Bois de Boulogne
With a heart as heavy as lead,
She wished that she was dead,
She had lost her maidenhead.
Her heart in a funk and covered with spunk,
Her knickers were torn and her cunt was worn,
She's the girl that lowered the price at Monte Carlo.
As he walked along the Bois de Boulogne
With his prick upon the stand,
The girls all say it's grand
To take it in their hand.
You give them a bod and they're on the job,
Pulling the foreskin over the knob
Of the man who broke the bank at Monte Carlo.

XXV. THE VIRGIN STURGEON
Caviare comes from the virgin sturgeon.
   The male sturgeon is a very fine dish,
The virgin sturgeons need no urgin',
   That's why caviare is my dish.
I fed caviare to my girl-friend,
   She was a virgin tried and true,
Now that virgin needs no urgin',
   There's not a thing that she won't do.
I took my girl-friend to a surgeon,
   Just to see what he could do.
Said that surgeon, "She's no virgin.
   Where's the cash, or no-can-do."
Shad roe comes from a harlot shadfish,
   Shadfish faced a sorry fate,
A pregnant shadfish is a sad fish,
   He gets that way without a mate.
Oysters are prolific bivalves,
   They have young ones in their shell,
How they piddle is a riddle,
   But they do—so what the hell!
The green sea-turtle's mate is happy
   O'er her lover's winning ways:
First he grips 'er with his flipper
   Then he flips for days and days.
The lady clam is optimistic,
   Shoots her eggs out in the sea,
She hopes her suitor, as a shooter,
   Hits the self-same spot as she.
Give a thought to the canny codfish,
   Ever there when duty calls.
The female codfish is an odd fish,

From her too come codfish balls.
The trout is but a little salmon,
   Just half-grown and minus scales,
Yet the trout, just like the salmon,
   Can't get on without his tails.
Lucky creatures are the rayfish
   When a litter they essay.
Yes, my hearties, they have parties
   In the good old-fashioned way.

XXVI. BLINDED BY SHIT
There was an old lady who lived down our street,
    She got constipation through too much to eat;
She took Beecham's pills on a Saturday night
    And quickly she found that she wanted to shite.
Too-ra-la, too-ra-lay.
    Oh a rolling stone gathers no moss, so they say.
Too-ra-lay, too-ra-lit
    It's a bloody fine song but it's all about shit.
She went to the window and stuck out her arse
    At the moment a night watchman happened to pass;
He heard a strange noise as he gazed up on high
    Then a bloody great turd hit him straight in the eye.
Too-ra-la &c.
He looked to the North, he looked to the South,
    And a bloody big lump landed right in his mouth;
He looked to the East, he looked to the West
    As a further consignment arrived on his chest.
Too-ra-la &c.
The next time you walk over Westminster Bridge
    Look out for an old man asleep on the edge.
His chest bears a placard and on it is writ:
    "Be kind to an old man that's blinded by shit."
Too-ra-la &c.

XXVII. MY LOVE IS FOR A BOLD MARINE

A miner coming home one night
    Found his house without a light,
And as he went upstairs to bed
    A strange thought came into his head
He went into his daughter's room
    And found her hanging from a beam,
He took his knife and cut her down
    And on her breast this note he found.
"My love is for a bold marine,
    I always, always think of him.
And though he's far across the sea,
    He never, never thinks of me!"
"So all you maidens bear in mind,
    A good man's love is hard to find.
Dig my grave both wide and deep
    And rest my weary bones in sleep."
They dug her grave both wide and deep
    And laid white lilies at her feet,
On her breast a turtle dove
    To signify she died of love.

XXVIII. SONIA SNELL

This is the tale of Sonia Snell
   To whom an accident befell,
An accident, as will be seen,
   Embarrassing in the extreme.
It happened, as it does to many,
   That Sonia went to spend a penny
And entered with a modest grace
   The properly appointed place.
There at the back of the railway station
   She sat in silent meditation,
But sad to say she did not know
   The seat had been varnished an hour ago.
Poor Sonia soon came to realise
   Her inability to rise,
Although she struggled, pulled and yelled
   She found that she was firmly held.
She raised her voice in mournful shout,
   "Please, someone, come and get me out!"
Her cries for help very quickly brought
   A crowd of every kind and sort.
   "Gor blimey," said an ancient porter,
"We oughter soak 'er orf wiv water."
   The station-master and his staff
Were most polite and did not laugh;
   They tugged at Sonia's hands and feet
But could not shift her off the seat.
   A carpenter arrived at last
And finding Sonia still stuck fast
   Remarked "I know what I can do!"
And neatly sawed the seat in two.
   Sonia arose, only to find
She'd a wooden halo on behind,
   But an ambulance drove down the street

    And bore her off complete with seat.
They took the wooden-bustled gal
    Off quickly to the hospital
And seizing her by hands and head
    Laid her face down upon a bed.
The doctors came and cast their eyes
    Upon the seat with some surprise.
A surgeon said: "Upon my word,
    Could anything be more absurd?
Have any of you, I implore,
    Seen anything like this before?"
"Yes," cried a student, unashamed,
    "Frequently—but never framed!"

XXIX. LITTLE JIM

Now here's a pretty little song so listen if you will
About a little fellow born one night on Tooting Hill,
He was born on Tooting Hill my boys, but spawned in
    [Camberwell,
And when he popped out he gave a shout "My Old Man
    [fucked her well!"
Little Jim, content with masturbation,
Little Jim, playing with his tool,
Little Jim, content with simple frigging,
Thought a cunt was something you were called at public
    [school.
Now down at Egham Manor there was a great ado,
For he buggered all the prefects and all the masters too,
But finally he was expelled or so the records say,
For tossing off the Prince of Hales on Coronation Day.
Little Jim &c
Now Jenny was a whore in good old Cambridge town,
Who had gamahuched the Proctor while he wore his cap

[and gown;
So his Uncle wrote to Jimmy saying "Quick, and pack
　　[your things,
For the cunting season opens at the Twelfth at Kings!"
Little Jim &c
His arrival at the 'Varsity was really quite grotesque,
For he laid his penis down upon his tutor's desk;
Said his tutor "If the beastly thing drops off at an early date
Please send it. I should like it as a special paper-weight."
Little
Then he went to live with Milly where he began to find
That all his pals were queueing up for what they called a
　　['grind',
So down beneath the bed he lay despite the awful smell,
And every time a client came, young Jimmy came as well.
Little Jim &c
And Milly's all a landlord's daughter will or ought to be,
She rubs her Aunt each morning while she drinks a cup
　　[of tea;
He's been through her so many times, the magistrate
　　[declares,
That her vagina constitutes a legal thoroughfare.
Little Jim &c

XXX. MY JENNY WREN BRIDE
I've just come away from a wedding,
    And lor'—I could laugh till I died.
I'll never forget the relations I met
    When I married my Jenny Wren bride.
Her father, he works in the dockyard,
    Her brother, he owns a marine store,
And as for their habits, why talk about rabbits—
    They've got half the dockyard ashore.
When I asked her old man for a dowry
    He gave me a drum of soft soap,
A bundle of waste and some polishing paste
    And fifty-two fathoms of rope.
The present we had from her brother
    Was twenty-eight yards of Blue Jean;
Her brother, the Crusher, he gave us notepaper,
    Six packets of "Service Latrine".
Her relations hung flags in the churchyard
    And painted the archway with flatting,
When along came the bride they piped "over the side"
    And she tripped on the coconut matting.
Her wedding dress lashed up with spunyani
    Was made from an old cutter's sail,
On the top of her head a deck-cloth was spread
    And a spud-net in front for a veil.
Her petticoat made of black hessian,
    Her knickers cut out of green baize,
While for a suspender a motor-boat's fender
    And two pusser's gaiters for stays.
The bulk of the congregation
    Was made up of Wrens on the dole
While asleep in the back pew was a six-inch gun's crew
    And half of the standing patrol.
The parson strode up to the altar

And asked "Who gives this woman away?"
A bloke from the *Hood* whispered "Blimey, I could,
   But let every dog have its day."
So now I'm just off on my honeymoon,
   I don't know what happens tonight,
But I've talked to a few who say that they do
   And they swear she's a bit of all-right!

XXXI. THE CHORIC SONG OF THE MASTURBATORS

Air: Finiculi Finicula
Last night,
   I pulled me pud:
It did me good,
   I knew it would.
Sling it,
   Fling it,'
Throw it on the floor,
   Smash it,
Crash it,
   Catch it in the door,
Some people say
   That fuckin's mighty good,
But for personal enjoyment,
   I'd rather pull me pud.

XXXII. THREE OLD WHORES FROM WINNIPEG

Air: 'My Love Lies Dying'.
Three old whores from Winnipeg
Were drinking sherry wine,
One said to the other,
"Your hole's no bigger'n mine."
"You'r a liar," said the other one,
"For mine's as big as the sea.
The ships sail in and the ships sail out,
And never bother me."
"You're a liar," said the other one,
"For mine's as big the air,
The ships sail in and the ships sail out,
And never tickle a hair."
"You're a liar," said the other one,
"For mine's as big as the moon.
The ships sail in on the first 'o the year
And don't come out till June."
"You're all three liars," said the very first one,
"For mine's the biggest of all.
The ships sail in, and the fleets sail in,
And never come out at all,"

XXXIII. TALE ONE
Brisk Friar John, a merry weight,
His convent's pride and convent's height,
With rosy cheeks and double chin,
To kiss a wench he thought no sin:
The midnight hour, th'appointment made,
To uncase his holy masquerade,
Obedient to his silent call,
The zealous votary climbed the wall.
From virtue drawn by him astray,
Through a barred window screws her way.
Friar John: Take not my dear these rubs amiss,
For narrow is the road to bliss.
Welcome thou paragon of charms,
And haste into my loving arms!
Entered, he lays her quickly down,
She, soon as covered by his gown,
With drawling voice and rolling eyes,
Wriggling addresses to the skies.
Maid: Under thy shadow Lord I lie,
O grant me but Fertility!
'Twas then the Prior walked his round,
Stopped as he heard a rustling sound—

Taps at the door, cries *"Benedicte,*
What noise disturbs tranquillity?"
Friar John: The Devil incarnate's here within,
And fain would tempt poor John to sin.
Prior: Then drive the infernal beast away,
Five *Paters* and ten *Aves* say.
Friar John: I have heard and conned my beads—nay more,
With Holy Water drowned the floor,

To make grim Satan sooner part,
And vent the ardour of my heart,
I have ejaculations made!
"God bless your work," the Prior said.

XXXIV. TALE TWO
Tell me, friend John—do, if you can,
What is the reason, if a man
Attempts to take a Lady fair,
By you know what, lies you know where,
That while he lives he still shall find,
The female, be she cross or kind
Fret, frown, and push his hand away?
Tell me the reason, tell me pray.
Women still make a great pretence,
To modesty and innocence.
And about virtue make a rout,
This is the reason without doubt.
Listen, you shall the reason know;
Whene'er you thrust your hand below,
All women be they foul or fair,
Know that a hand is useless there;
But if from Mayday to December
You offer there the proper member,
Push as you will to give them pain
They'll neither wince—nor yet complain.

XXXV. TALE THREE
An Alderman, a wealthy cit,
One morning met a man of wit;
Dear Dick—said he—I like your way
You're always cheerful, every day.
Come dine with me, I know what's what
And have three daughters, mum of that.
And Dick—he said—to tell the truth,
Thou art a most bewitching youth,
Whate'er you do with ease is done,
I wish I had you for a son:
I wish Dear Richard you'd agree,
To take a wife out of my three.
Dick, at this strange discourse amazed
Upon the blushing sisters gazed.
The smiling maidens owned for truth,
They had no quarrel with the youth.
Dear Sir—said Dick—I cannot tell
I love them all so very well,
But if their wit you'll let me try
I'll soon find out the mystery.
Just let each maid keep up her mask
Till one single question ask.
Whether the mouth that's in your face
Or that in a more hidden place
The eldest is?
Who answers best
Shall triumph in my happy breast.

The first born daughter said
"In truth I think the eldest is my mouth,
Since in it there are teeth of bone,
In that below, I'm sure are none."
The second said, "The seat of love

Is eldest, for the mouth above,
Upon its lips no hair can show,
But I have got a beard below."
The youngest sister, smiling, said,
"I am a young and silly maid,
But yet I think the mouth above
Is elder than the seat of love.
And what I say I thus evince,
My upper mouth was weaned long since
And flesh and fish and bone can eat,
But my mouth below longs for the teat."
Richard on this embraced the fair
And for the youngest did declare:
He married her with great content,
And never did his choice repent.

XXXVI. SHE WENT FOR A RIDE IN A MORGAN

She went for a drive in a Morgan,
    She sat with the driver in front.
He fooled with her genital organs:
    The more vulgar-minded say "cunt".
Now she had a figure ethereal,
    She auctioned it out to mens' cocks,
And contracted diseases venereal:
    The more vulgar-minded say "pox".
The dazzling peak of perfection,
    There wasn't a prick she would scorn,
She gave every man an erection:
    The more vulgar-minded say "horn".
Did you ever see Anna make water?
    It's a sight that you ought not to miss.
She can leak for a mile and a quarter:
    The more vulgar-minded say "piss".
If I had two balls like a bison
    And a prick like a big buffalo,
I would sit on the edge of creation
    And piss on the buggers below.

XXXVII. DOWN BY THE BARRACK GATE

At the call of the last trumpet,
    Stood a little strumpet.
    Down by the barrack gate.
Some private from the kitchen,
    Brought that dirty little bitch in,
    Down by the barrack gate.
Said that martinet the Colonel,
    "Damn my soul in fires infernal,
    The joys of fornication,
Are for those of higher station.
    It's the pastime of the great!"
But the Sergeant drill instructor,
    Took her down the road and fucked her,
    Down by the barrack gate.
How that little harlot giggled,
    And her chubby arsecheeks wriggled,
    For the Sergeant fucked like three men,
Spilling pints and pints of semen.
    Down by the barrack gate.
But now his penis itches,
    In his regimental britches,
    And he sheds an amber tear,
    Sympathetic gonorrhea,
    Down by the barrack gate.

XXXVIII. POOR BLIND NELL

The sun shone on the village green,
  It shone on Poor Blind Nell,
But did she see the sun that shone?
  Did she fucking 'ell!
A sailor to the village came,
  The captain of a lugger,
He captivated Poor Blind Nell,
  The dirty, lousy bugger.
One night he slept with Poor Blind Nell,
  He knew it wasn't lawful,
And though her tits were very sweet
  Her feet smelt fucking awful.
He took the girl out in a punt
  And to the seat he lashed 'er,
Then lacerated Poor Nell's cunt,
  The dirty, lousy bastard.
And when he went to sea again
  He sent her books and parcels,
But did he write and thank Poor Nell?
  Did he fucking arseholes!

XXXIX. THE STREET OF A THOUSAND ARSEHOLES

In the street of A Thousand Arseholes,
By the sign of the swinging tit,
There stands a Chinese maiden,
By the name of Hu Flung Shit.
Sweet as the scented lotus,
With eyes like pools of piss,
She lies there in the gutter,
Whanking with celestial bliss.
As she dreams of her love—the bastard,
As she longs for his throbbing rod,
As she marks her score along the floor—
Up walks Scro Turn Sod.
"Come fly with me my purse of spunk,"
He hollered prick in hand,
"My stand for you will last weeks through,
Like snow on the Gobi sand."
She lifted up her starboard tit,
And wisely scratched her snatch,
Then looked at him with a split-arsed grin,
And said "Go fuck a Mandarin."
He clutched his prick with cow-like mit,
And smashed it 'gainst the walls,
Took off his hat and fucked at that,
Then danced upon his balls.
At last his anger mastered him,
He pissed himself with rage,
He went and shit, and stamped in it,
And his foreskin went quite beige.
Emotion quite o'ercame him,
He fell—just like a sack,
And she stood on him with a serene grin,
And pissed on the fucker's back.

The Chinese maiden whanks no more,
She arose and took on shit,
In the street of A Thousand Arseholes
'Neath the sign of the Swinging Tit.

XXXX. I DON'T WANT TO JOIN THE ARMY

I don't want to join the army,
I don't want to go to war,
I just want to wander round
Piccadilly Underground,
Livin' off the life of an high priced Lady!
I don't want a bayonet up my arsehole,
I don't want my bollocks shot away,
I'd sooner live in England,
Not-so-merry England,
And fuck all my living days away!

XXXXI. LITTLE SALLY

Little Sally based her hopes
   On a book by Marie Stopes;
But to judge from her condition
   She must have bought the wrong edition.
All the sprays that ever whirled
   Cannot clean this wicked world
Of the over-population
   Caused by careless copulation.
All the choicest goods of France
   Cannot beat the laws of Chance.
Better by far to trust to luck
   And so enjoy an honest fuck.

XXXXII. THE FARMER'S DOG

A farmer's dog once came to town
   Whose Christian name was Pete,
His pedigree was ten yards long,
   His looks were hard to beat.
As he trotted down the road
   It was beautiful to see
His work on every corner,
   His mark on every tree.
He watered every gateway,
   He never missed a post,
For piddling was his masterpiece
   And piddling was his boast.
The city dogs stood looking on
   With deep and jealous rage
To see this simple country dog,
   The piddler of the age.
They smelt him over, one- by one,
   They smelt him two by two;

The noble Pete in high disdain
    Stood still till they were through.
And as they sniffed him over
    Their praise for him ran high,
But when one sniffed him underneath
    Pete piddled in his eye.
Then just to show these city dogs
    He didn't give a damn,
Pete strolled into a grocer's shop
    And piddled on some ham.
He piddled on the onions,
    He piddled on the floor,
And when the grocer kicked him out
    Pete piddled on the door.
Behind him all the city dogs
    Debated what to do—
They'd hold a piddling carnival
    And show him who was who!
They showed Pete all the piddling posts
    They knew about the town,
They started out with many winks
    To get this stranger down.
But Pete was with them every trick,
    With vigour and with vim,
A thousand piddles more or less
    Were all the same to him.
And on and on went noble Pete,
    With hind leg kicking high,
While most were lifting legs in bluff
    Or piddling mighty dry.
And on and on went noble Pete
    And watered every sandhill
Till all the city champions
    Were piddled to a standstill.

Then Pete an exhibition gave
    In all the ways to piddle,
Like double drips and fancy flips
    And now and then a dribble.
While all the time the country dog
    Did neither wink nor grin,
But piddled blithely out of town
    As he had piddled in.
The city dogs said: "So long, Pete,
    Your piddling did defeat us."
But no one ever put them wise
    That Pete had diabetes.

XXXXIII. I DREAMED MY LOVE

I dreamed my love lay in her bed:
    It was my chance to take her:
Her legs and arms abroad were spread:
    She slept, I dare not wake her.
O pity it were that one so fair
    Should crown her love with willow;
The tresses of her golden hair,
Did kiss her lonely pillow.
    Methought her belly was a hill
Much like a mount of pleasure,
Under whose brow there grows a well,
    Whose depth no man can measure.
About the pleasant mountain top,
    There grows a lovely thicket,
Wherein my two hounds traveled,
    And raised a lively prickett.
They hunted there with pleasant noise,
    About the ferny mountain,
'Til heat the prickett forced to fly,

    And skip into the fountain.
The hounds they followed to the brink,
    And there at him they barked,
He plunged about but would not shrink,
    His coming forth they waited.
Then forth he came as one half lame,
    Limp, weary, faint and tired,
And laid him down between her legs,
    For help he had required.
The hounds they were refreshed again,
    My love from sleep returned,
And dreamed she held me in her arms,
    And she was not alarmed.

XXXXIV. THE COWPUNCHER'S WHORE

Way down in Alberta
    Where the bullshit grows thick,
Where folks chew tobacco
    And the cowboys come quick,
There lives young Charlotte
    The girl I adore,
The pride of the prairie,
    The cowpunchers' whore.
One day on the prairie
    While whittlin' a stick
I was riding along,
    With a throb in my prick,
When who should I meet
    But the girl I adore,
Charlotte, the harlot
    The cowpunchers' whore.
She's dirty, she's vulgar,

    She shits in the street,
Whenever you meet her
    She's always on heat,
She'll fuck for a dollar,
    Take less or take more,
Charlotte, the harlot
    The cowpunchers' whore.
One day in a canyon,
    She opened her quim,
A rattlesnake saw her,
    And flung himself in,
Now Charlotte gives
    The cowpunchers a fright,
The only cunt in Alberta
    That rattles and bites.
A lusty cowpuncher
    From down Texas way,
Took out his six-shooter
    And started to play,
He tickled her cunt
    With a forty-five shell,
And the rattlesnake died
    Saying "What fucking hell!"

XXXXV. ARSEHOLES ARE CHEAP TODAY
Air: La Dona E Mobile
Arseholes are cheap today,
Cheaper than yesterday,
Small boys are half-a-crown,
Standing up or lying down,
Big ones for bigger pricks,
Biggest ones cost three-and-six,
Get yours before they're gone,
Come now and try one.

XXXXVI. OLLIE, OLLIE, OLLIE
Ollie, Ollie, Ollie,
With his balls on a trolley
And his cock tied up in string,
Sitting on the grass
With a bugle up his arse,
Trying to play "The King".

XXXXVII. THE RAJAH OF ASTRAKAN
There was a Rajah of Astrakan, Yo Ho!
　　A most licentious cunt of a man,
Yo Ho! Of wives he had a hundred and nine
　　Including his favourite concubine. *Yo Ho!*
You buggers, Yo Ho!
　　You buggers, Yo Ho! Yo Ho!
One day he had the hell of a stand,
　　So he called a warrior, one of his band:
"Go down to my harem, you lazy swine,
　　And fetch my favourite concubine."
Yo Ho! You buggers &c.
The warrior fetched the concubine,
　　A figure like Venus, a face divine,
The Rajah gave a significant grunt
　　And parked his prick inside her cunt.
Yo Ho! You buggers &c.
The Rajah's strokes were loud and long,
　　The maiden answered sure and strong,
But just when the ride had come to a head
　　They both fell through the fucking bed.
Yo Ho! You buggers &c.
They hit the floor with the hell of a dunt
　　Which completely buggered the poor girl's cunt,
And as for the Rajah's magnificent cock—
　　It never recovered from the shock.
Yo Ho! You buggers &c.
There is a moral to this tale,
　　There is a moral to this tale.
If you would fuck a girl at all
　　Stick her right up against the wall.
Yo Ho! You buggers &c.

XXXXVIII. NIGHTFUCK
Air: D'ye Ken John Peel.

Cats on the rooftops,
    Cats on the tiles,
Cats with syphillis,
    Cats with piles,
Cats with their arseholes
    Wreathed in smiles,
As they revel in the joys of copulation.
The Donkey is a lonely bloke,
    Very, very rarely
Gets in a poke,
    But when he does,
He lets it soak
    For he revels in the joy of copulation.
The hippopotamus so it seems,
    Only occasionally
Has wet dreams, '
    But when he does
O! It comes in streams,
    For he revels in the joys of copulation.
Long-nosed parsons
    Jump like goats;
Pale-faced maidens
    Fuck like stoats,
And the whole bloody world
    Looks on and gloats,
As they revel in the joys of copulation.
The Ostrich on the moor
    Is a solitary chick
It never gets a chance to
    Dip its wick
But whenever he does
    It goes in thick
For he revels in the joys of copulation.
The Regimental Sergeant Major

Leads a miserable life,
He can't afford a mistress,
　　And he hasn't got a wife,
So the stuffs it up the arsehole
　　Of the Regimental Fife,
As he revels in the joys of copulation.
When you wake up in the morning,
　　Feeling full of sexual joy,
And your wife's a trifle musty
　　And your daughter's rather coy,
Then stuff it up the turdpipe
　　Of your favourite boy,
As you revel in the joys of copulation.
When you find yourself at evening
　　With the devil of a stand,
From the pressure of the urine
　　On your seminary gland,
If there ain't a woman handy
　　Use your own fair randy hand,
As you revel in the joys of masturbation.

XXXXIX. THE HARLOT OF JERUSALEM
In days of yore there lived a whore,
A prostitute of lewd repute,
A jade who did a roaring trade,
The Harlot of Jerusalem!
   Hi, Yi, Cathusalem, Cathusalem, Cathusalem,
   Hi, Yi, Cathusalem, the Harlot of Jerusalem.
A student lived hard by the wall,
Who, though he only had one ball,
Had been through very nearly all
The Harlots of Jerusalem!
Hi, Yi &c.
One night returning from a spree,
With customary cunt-lust he,
Although he only had one dong,
Called on the fair Cathusalem!
Hi, Yi &c.
It was for her no piece of luck
This lusty lad should need a fuck,
And chose her cunt from out the rut,
Of harlots in Jerusalem!
Hi, Yi &c.
For though he paid his women well,
This syphilitic spawn of hell,
Struck down each year and sorely fell,
Ten harlots of Jerusalem!
Hi, Yi &c.
Forth from the town he took the slut,
For 'twas his pleasant whim to fuck,
By the Salvation Army's hut,
The love of pure Jerusalem.
Hi, Yi &c.
And heaving reached this shady nook,
Forth from its hiding place he took,

His penis twisted like a crook,
The pride of foul Jerusalem!
Hi, Yi &c.
He placed his whore against a tree,
And tied her at the leg and knee,
For he knew there the strain would be,
Upon the Fair Cathusalem!
Hi, Yi &c.
He gripped her tight around the bum,
And squirted like a gatling gun,
And sowed the seed of many a son,
Within the fair Cathusalem!
Hi, Yi &c.
It was a sight to make you sick,
To hear him grunt so fast and thick,
Exploring with his hooked prick,
The womb of Fair Cathusalem!
Hi, Yi &c.
Then up there came an Onanite,
Whose balls were melons made of shite,
Who swore that he would gaol that night
The Harlot of Jerusalem!
Hi, Yi &c.
He loathed the vice of fornication,
For his delight was masturbation,
And exposing to the Nation,
The whores of old Jerusalem!
Hi, Yi &c.
So when he saw the fucking pair,
With Holy rage he rent the air,
And said he'd have their pubic hair,
To show off to the Nation!
Hi, Yi &c.
A tree supplied him with a stick,

To which he fastened half a brick,
And he took a swipe at the mighty prick,
Of the student of Jerusalem.
Hi, Yi &c.
He seized the fucker by his hook,
And such a mighty heave he took,
He flung him over Kendron's brook,
That babbles past Jerusalem!
Hi, Yi &c.
The student with a mighty roar,
Returned to grapple with the bore,
And with his flaming jack did score,
That arsehole of Jerusalem!
Hi, Yi &c.
And feeling full of rage and fight,
He flung the bloody Onanite,
And rubbed his nose in Cathy's shite,
The sweetest in Jerusalem.
Hi, Yi &c.
The wily strumpet knew her part,
She pissed her cunt and blew a fart,
And broke the Onanite apart,
With stinks of Old Jerusalem!
Hi, Yi &c.
As for the student and his lass,
Many a gallon of sperm they passed,
Until she joined the V.D. class,.
For harlots in Jerusalem!
Hi, Yi &c.

L. DIAMOND LILY
Air: The Road To The Isles
There's a man that sits in prison
   With his hands upon his knees,
And the shadow of his penis on the wall;
   And the hairs go flicker-flacker,
From his arsehole to his knacker,
   And the rats are playing croquet
     With his balls.
There's a Gentleman's urinal,
   To the North of Waterloo,
There's a Ladies' just a little further down,
   There's a constipated woman,
Putting pennies in the slot,
   While the attendant stands
     And watches with a frown.
Oh my name is Diamond Lily,
   I'm a whore in Piccadilly,
And my Father runs a brothel in the Strand,
   And my brother sells his arsehole
To the Guards at Windsor Castle,
We're the finest fuckin' family
   In the land.

LI. THE KEYHOLE IN THE DOOR
I left the party early, just after half-past nine,
And as I had expected her room was next to mine,
So like a bold Columbus I set out to explore
And took up my position by the keyhole in the door.
   Oh the keyhole in the door my boys,
   The keyhole in the door;
   I took up my position by
   The keyhole in the door.

She first took off her slippers, her dainty feet to show,
And then her cami-knickers to reveal her so-and-so.
"Now take off all you've got, my dear," was all I could
   [implore,
And silently as possible I crossed the threshold door.
Oh the keyhole in the door my boys, &c.
Silently I closed the door and took her in my arms
And rather unexpectedly discovered all her charms,
But in case some other fellow should see the sights I saw
I hung her cami-knickers o'er the keyhole in the door.
Oh the keyhole in the door my boys, &c.
That night I rode in glory, and other things besides,
On her lily-white belly I had many glorious rides,
But when I woke next morning my tool it was so sore
I thought that I'd been fucking up the keyhole in the door.
Oh the keyhole in the door my boys, &c.

LII. THE TRAVELIN' MAN
When I got home on Saturday night as drunk as a cunt
   [can be,
I saw a hat upon the rack where my old hat should be,
So I said to the wife, the pride o' me life,
Why aren't you true to me, whose is the hat upon the rack,
   Where my old hat should be?
   "Oh you're drunk you cunt
   You silly old cunt,
   You're as drunk as a cunt can be,
   That's not a hat upon the rack
   But a chamber-pot you see."
In all the miles I've traveled a million miles or more,

A chamber pot with a hat-band on I never have seen
    [before.
I saw a head upon the bed where my old head should be:
    "That's not a head upon the bed,
    But a baby's bum you see."
A baby's bum with whiskers on I never did see before.
I saw a nob betwixt her legs where my old nob should be:
    "That's not a nob betwixt my legs
    But a rolling pin you see"
A rolling pin with balls attached I never have seen before.
I saw a mess on her nightdress where my old mess should
    [be:
"That's not a mess upon my dress,
But some clotted cream you see."
Some clotted cream that smelt of fish I never have smelt
    [before.
Note: only the first stanza set out for singing.

LIII. PLEASE DONT BURN OUR SHITHOUSE DOWN

Please don't burn our shithouse down,
    Mother is willin' to pay;
Father's a sailin' the high seas,
    And Nell's in a family way.
My brother dear has gonorrhea,
    Don't make us shit in the rain;
Little Bill has got the run,
    And he wants to go there again.
Please don't burn our shithouse down,
    For times is fuckin' hard,
And if you burn the old thing down,
    We'll have to shit in the yard.

LIV. TIM THE TINKER

The Lady of the Manor,
Was dressing for the Ball,
When she saw a Highland Tinker
Pissing up against the wall.
With his bloody great kidney wiper,
And his balls the size of three,
And a yard-and-a-half of foreskin.
Hanging down below his knee.
The Lady wrote a letter,
And in it she did say,
She'd rather be fucked by a tinker,
Than his Lordship any day.
With his &c.
The Tinker got the letter,
And when it he did read,
His balls began to fester,

And his prick began to bleed.
With his &c.
He mounted on his donkey,
And to her place did ride,
With his prick over his shoulder,
And his balls strapped to his side.
With his &c.
He fucked them in the parlour,
He fucked them in the Hall,
The butler cried "Gawd Sive Us,
For he wants to fuck us all."
With his &c.
He fucked the Groom in the parlour,
And the Duchess in her pew,
But then he fucked the butler,
And the butler's pet mole too.
With his &c.
Some say the Tinker's gone now,
Gone fucking down to hell,
All set to fuck the Devil
And we hope he does it well.
With his &c.

LV. THE GREAT FARTING CONTEST
I'll tell you a ditty that's certain to please,
Of the great farting contest at Shittem-On-Peas,
When all the best arses parade in a field,
To match in fair contest for a large silver shield.
Some lift up their arses and fart up the scale,
To compete for a cup and a barrel of ale,
While others whose arses are biggest and strangest,
Compete in a section for loudest and longest.
Now this Easter evening had drawn a huge crowd,
And the betting was even on Mrs. McLoud,
For it had appeared in the evening edition,
That this lady's arse was in perfect condition.
Now old Mrs. Jones had a perfect backside,
With bunches of hair and a wart on each side,
She fancied her chances of winning with ease,
Having trained herself well on cabbage and peas.
Mrs. Bindley arrived with a roar of applause,
And promptly began to pull off her drawers,
For though she'd no chance in the fucking display,
She'd the sweetest young arse you'd see any day.
I found Mr. Pothole was backed for a place,
Though he'd lately been placed in the deepest disgrace,
For farting so loud that it drowned the church organ,
And gassed the young Vicar and the choir-boy Morton.
The Canon arrived and ascended the stand,
And addressed a few words to this gazeous band.
He read then the rules as displayed in the bills,
Forbidding injections and usage of pills.
The contestants lined up for the signal to start,
And winning the toss Mrs. Jones blew first fart,
The crowd stood agasp in silence and wonder,
And the B.B.C. gave a warning of thunder.
Then young Mr. Pothole was called to the front,

And began to perform a remarkable stunt,
With legs opened wide and tightly clenched hands,
He blew off the roof of the Royal Grandstands.
But Mrs. McLoud reckoned nothing with this,
She'd had some weak tea and was all wind and piss;
She took up her stance and opponents defied,
But unluckily shat—and was disqualified.
Next came Mrs. Bingle who shyly appeared,
And smiled on the crowd who lustily cheered.
They thought she- was pretty—but no farting runt,
And most of the crowd wished to look at her cunt.
But with hands on her hips she stood farting alone,
And the crowd was amazed at the sweetness of tone.
The judges agreed without stopping to think,
"First prize Mrs. Bingle—oh she's starting to stink!"
She walked to the dais with maidenly gait,
And took with a fart the set of gold plate;
She turned to the crowd as they started to sing,
And with her sweet arse burbled God Save The Queen.

LVI. NO BALLS AT ALL
Oh gather round lovers and listen to me;
I'll tell you a tale that will fill you with glee;
There was a young maiden—so pretty and small;
She married a man who had no balls at all.
Balls, balls,
  No balls at all,
A very short penis,
  And no balls at all!
The night they were married, they crept into bed...
Her cheeks they were rosy, her lips they were red...
She felt for his penis—his penis was small...
She felt for his balls, he had no balls at all!
Balls &c.
Oh Mother dear Mother, O what can I do?
I've married a man who's unable to screw,
There is not another with penis as small!
Moreover my husband has no balls at all.
Balls &c.
Oh Daughter, sweet Daughter, do not be too sad,
The very same trouble I had with your Dad.
There's many a rounder who'll answer the call,
Of the wife of the man who has no balls at all!
Balls &c.
This pretty sad maiden took Mother's advice:
She found the procedure exceedingly nice!
A bouncing big baby was born in the fall:
The poor little bastard had no balls at all!
Balls &c.

LVII. ALL THE NICE GIRLS
All the nice girls love a candle,
All the nice girls love a wick,
For there's something about a candle,
That's just like a young man's prick,
Nice and greasy, goes in easy,
Its a lady's pride and joy,
Its been up the Queen of Spain,
And its going up again,
Ship ahoy! It's a boy!

LVIII. THERE WAS A PRIEST
There was a priest a dirty beast,
His name was Alexander,
He had a prick ten inches thick,
And called it his commander.
One night he met a gypsy maid,
Her face was black as charcoal,
And in the dark he missed his mark,
And shoved it up her arsehole.
A babe was born one sunny morn,
Its face was black as charcoal,
It had a prick ten inches thick,
And a double-barrelled arsehole.

LIX. DEAD-EYE DICK AGAIN
This is the tale of Dead-Eye Dick,
He was the man with the corkscrew prick,
He searched the world on a fruitless hunt,
To find a girl with a corkscrew cunt.
And when he found her he dropped dead,
Because she had a left hand thread.

LX. SALOME
Now, down our street we had a crashing party,
Everybody there was so gay and hearty,
Talk about a treat, we wolfed up all the meat,
Drank all the beer in the boozer down the street.
There was Old Uncle Jo, fairly fucked up,
We put him in the cellar with the bulldog pup,
And little Sonny Jim tryin' to get it in,
With his arsehole winkin' at the moon!
    O Salome! Salome!
    You should see Salome!
    Dancing there
    With her tits all bare,
    Every little wriggle
    Makes the boys all stare.
    She swings it,
    She flings it,
    And the boys all murmur 'O'
    Take her around
    Lay her on the ground,
    Down where the roses grow!
She's a great big cow, twice the size o' me
Hairs on her fanny like the branches of a tree
She can run, jump, fight, shite, suck and fuck
Push a barrow wheel, a truck—that's my Salome.

On a Monday night I shove it up the back;
Tuesday night she takes it in the crack;
Every Wednesday she takes a spell,
On Thursday night she fucks like bloody hell.
Friday evening up her snout it goes,
In between her fingers, down between her toes,
And all day long she guzzles on my dong,
All day Saturday and Sunday!
    O Salome! O Salome!
    That's my girl Salome!
    Standing there
    With her arse all bare,
    Waiting with a stare
    To shove it right up there,
Slide it,
Glide it
Up her hungry cunt
Two swollen balls
And a gallon of best spunk,
That's my girl Salome!

LXI. THE BRICKLAYERS' UNION

When the bricklayer's union struck,
    Dear Old Bill was having a fuck,
Now by union rules he had to down tools,
    That's what I call bad luck.

LXII. ABDUL ABULBUL EMIR

In the Harems of Egypt, close-guarded and secret,
    The women are fairest of hair,
But the very best jerk is owned by a Turk
    Called Abdul Abulbul Emir.
A travelling brothel once came to the town,
    'Twas owned by a Shah from afar,
He issued a challenge to all who could fuck,
    'Gainst Ivan Skavinsky Skivar.
Old Abdul arrived with his bride by his side,
    He came in a bloody great car,
Bet a thousand gold lumps he'd shag many more rumps
    Than Ivan Skavinsky Skivar.
They met on a track with their tools hanging slack,
    The starter's gun punctured the air,
They were quick on the rise and folks gasped at the size
    Of Abdul Abulbul Emir.
All cunt hairs were shorn, no rubbers were worn,
    And Abdul's arse revved like a car,
But he hadn't a hope against the long even stroke
    Of Ivan Skavinsky Skivar.
When Ivan had won he was wiping his dong,
    He stooped down to polish his peer,.
He received a great root up his innocent shoot,
    From Abdul Abulbul Emir.
Now the cream of the joke when apart they were broke,
    Was laughed at for years by the Czar,
For Abdul the fool had busted his tool,
    In the arsehole of Ivan Skivar.

LXIII. THE ONE-EYED RILEY

Sitting in O'Riley's bar one day
Telling yarns of blood and slaughter,
Suddenly a thought came to my head,
Why not fuck O'Riley's daughter?
> *Yippee-I-aye, yippee-I-aye,*
> *Yippee-I-aye for the one-eyed Riley,*
> *Arseholes, rissoles, balls and all,*
> *Shove it up the nearest cunt!*

I took the fair girl by the hand,
Gently swung my left leg over,
Never a word the sweet child said,
Laughed like hell till the fun was over.
Yippee &c.
I heard a footstep on the stair,
Who could it be but the one-eyed Riley,
With two pistols in his hands,
Looking for the man who had fucked his daughter?
Yippee &c.
I grabbed O'Riley by the hair,
Shoved his hair in a tub o' water,
Stuffed his pistols up his arse,
Bloody sight quicker than I stuffed his daughter!
Yippee &c.

For those who have forgotten the melody it can be seen in the appendix to THE COCKTAIL PARTY by Mr. T. Eliot, the London playwright.

LXIV. LULU

NOTE: Music laid out as in original.

Some girls work in fact'ries some girls work in stores,
But my girl works in a knockin' shop with forty other
     [whores!

O bang away Lulu, bang away Lulu,
Bang away good and strong,
Whata we to do for a good blow through,
When Lulu's dead and gone?

Lulu had a baby, it was an awful shock,
She couldn't call it Lulu 'cos the bastard had a cock!
O bang away &c.

I took her to the pictures, we sat down in the stalls,
And every time the lights went out she grabbed me by the
     [balls!
O bang away &c.

She and I went fishing in a dainty punt,
And every time I hooked a sprat she stuffed it up her cunt!
O bang away &c.

I wish I was a silver ring upon my Lulu's hand,
And every time she scratched her arse I'd see the promised
          [land!
O bang away &c.

I wish I was a chamber pot under Lulu's bed,
And every time she took a piss I'd see her maidenhead!
O bang away &c.

LXV. FATHER'S GRAVE
They're diggin' up Father's grave to build a sewer:
    They're doin' this regardless of expense:
    They're shovelin' his remains,
    To make way for ten inch drains,
To ease the bums of some grand new residents.
Now what's the use of havin' a religion?
    If when you're dead troubles never cease?
    'Cos some society squit
    Wants a pipeline for his shit,
They won't let poor old Father rest in peace.
Now Father in his life was not a quitter,
    And I don't suppose he'll be a quitter now.
    And in his grey grave sheet
    He'll haunt the shit-house seat,
So's they won't be pleased to crap there anyhow.
And blimey! Won't there be some constipation?
    And won't those richies rant and rave and shout?
    And it'll serve them bloody right
    To have to bake their shite,
For fucking poor old Father's grave about!

COUNT PALMIRO VICARION'S BOOK OF LIMERICKS

FOREWORD

Bowing before the insistence of several friends, I am finally surrendering for publication some of my favourite limericks. Let me say at once that is has been no easy matter assembling these verses. For the limerick is usually found, or better still, *heard* in drawing rooms, sacristies, bawdy-houses, all-night bars, Common Rooms, and at parties where the hostess loses control of the company: in short in all the usual places where a sort of verbal tradition resides and a versifier may exist. Hence, a limerick, that very fugitive thing, has got to be memorized or hastily jotted on a bit of paper napkin, the back of a calling card, or even—as in the case of one of my best discoveries—on a square of toilet tissue. Either that, or it is lost, gone.

Inasmuch as dozens of collections of limericks already exist and the actual number of verses must run into the thousands, I must assume that the urgent requests for this particular collection spring from the wish to have a book in which each limerick is funny. Funny mine are, every one of them; at least to me. Acting with uncompromising ruthlessness, I have cruelly rejected hundreds of verses which did not meet the highest of standards—which did not strike *me* as witty or funny.

During those warm evenings, so long ago but so well-remembered, when that great fellow Douglas and I would swap limericks and trouble the Mediterranean air with our laughter, we would often dispute the sources, purpose, and criteria of excellence in the limerick. "Vicarion," he would say (he was correct at all times and never called me Palmiro), "Vicarion, you've got it all ass-backwards! The limerick comes to one like a gift from a pagan god; you must accept it, relish it, and of course, if possible, publish it!" (Even then I could not resist polishing a little, re-rhyming a bit or even borrowing a good idea and casting it into new forms.) Douglas had a reverence for the limerick which was admirable, equaled, I would say, by no one save the collector of that exquisite compilation of filth and fun, THE LIMERICK (published in Paris, 1953, by Les Hautes Etudes).

Nevertheless, I suspected that Douglas could relish a poor limerick because it offered such a fine springboard for the soarings of his whimsy: "Now, what the devil was that girl doing in Cawnpore in the first place!" he would add, turning a mediocre rhyme to his advantage. He would never touch the limerick itself, but would attach lines which might make it more amusing:.

There was a young man named Skinner
Who had a young lady to dinner.
At half past nine
They sat down to dine,
And by quarter of ten it was in her.
What, dinner? No Skinner!

But — the vital question —: is this extended witticism a limerick? The answer: no. Unfortunately, no. Nor is that masterpiece by Madame de L. de T., wife of the former governor of Indonesia,

There was a young man of Kilkankie
Who gathered his sperm in a hankie
Which he left on a seat
Female buttocks to meet

And that's how Jesus was born.
a specimen of the *genre*.

The limerick is a social grace of five lines rhymed twice (aabba) and, when excellent, impolite. The form was popularised in Victorian England by that timid genius, Edward Lear, as a children's amusement and introduction to verse-making. However, little is known of children's aptitude—their success or failure in this art—for the verse pattern so suited the adult intellect that parents speedily usurped the form and by 1900 the limerick had become naturally obscene.

Because of the terseness of its form, die most successful examples depend upon happy turns of phrase and superior rhyming. Hence, the limerick is usually the product of one man, or, given those rare circumstances wherein the noblest enterprises can be undertaken by like minds, four or five companions, seized by a rising determination, will round off a promising couplet with three more lines and thereby produce a triumphant conclusion.

On the other hand, the limerick is seldom heard to resound in pubs, factories, or in the mines. These localities rather favour the production of our great *dirty jokes* and ballads. The joke needing some length to be excellent, is rambling, almost epic in its style, whereas the limerick relies upon its rigorous form in order to be engaging. The limerick is in one sense fundamentally discreet: it is one man's joke—the individual's cleverness as opposed to collective, roistering, leather-lunged laughter at Man's less divine aspects. The best limerick recounted in prose remains very dull indeed until heightened by metre and rhyme. And this gives rise to the edict: *Never tell a Limerick if you are unsure of its lines.*

What then makes a limerick funny? Ah, a knotty question over which many a fine brain has puzzled and grown dazed. Unerring anapestic rhythm is essential, by all means. Beyond that, what is there to say? A formula for first lines appears to exist: "There was a young man (girl, boy, dog) from Calcutta (Peru, Madras, Bombay)"; (these areas are favoured because they afford the easiest rhymes). A recently observable trend among limericists, however, is their rejection of "There was a..." as an opening bar. Certainly this is to be applauded, though many reactionary—and they are amongst the best— composers will not tolerate what they consider to be a vulgarisation of a ritualistic element.

Intrinsic to its form is a certain magic in the limerick: any one of the five lines may contain the explosive climax— the high point or the low—but the fifth should bind them all together and in retrospect give them poignancy. A common pattern is a clever fourth line or one of startlingly inappropriate innocence thunderously corrected by a boisterous fifth line:

There was a young man from Devizes
Whose balls were of different sizes:
One ball was small,
Almost no ball at all —
But the other was large and won prizes.

Rarely will it occur that each line is hilarious—no art is exclusively composed of masterworks, but every art has them. I know of but one impeccable limerick, an extraordinary achievement by the editor of THE LIMERICK (a volume, by the way, so comprehensive that it seems to contain even those verses one supposed one had composed oneself).

"My back aches. My penis is sore.
I simply can't fuck any more.
I'm dripping with sweat,
And you haven't come yet:

And, my God, it's a quarter to four."

The rest of these pages offering the reader limericks only and no further intrusion by me, my remarks might perhaps close with some advice. Firstly, the limerick is precious, an exquisite thing, like a good Burgundy; it should not be taken indifferently; too often, or in unduly large quantities. Only a fool, I repeat, a fool would gulp down a glass of Chambertin or read this book at a sitting. Secondly, for the fullest enjoyment, a limerick is to be savoured in a group at just that pause in a conversation when, as though of its own accord, it can be spontaneously introduced, and then its effect is certain to be registered with fullest impact. Because of its form, the limerick is often thoroughly acceptable in our society where and when a joke might cause embarrassment or alarm.

Finally, a true limericist is prepared to hear a verse twice. Improved versions should be told in private to the *raconteur*. Anyone who interrupts the telling of a good limerick stamps himself as an unqualifiable bore.

I wish here to express thanks for the generous and cooperative attitudes of the R. Rev. T.S.E. of London, Mr. A. T. of Gambier, Ohio, Miss S. of *Trixies,* Port Said, and a host of other gentlefolk.

Count Palmiro Vicarion.
Alma Atta, January, 1955.

1

The team of Tom and Louise
Do an act in the nude on their knees.
They crawl down the aisle
While fucking dog-style,
And the orchestra plays Kilmer's "Trees."

2

Rosalind, a pretty young lass,
Had a truly magnificent ass:
Not rounded and pink
As you possibly think—
It was grey, had long ears, and ate grass.

3

There was a young lady of Exeter,
So pretty, that men craned their necks at her.
One went so far
As to wave from his car
The distinguishing mark of his sex at her.

4

If Leo your own birthday marks
You will fuck until 40, when starts
A new pleasure in stamps,
Boy Scouts and their camps,
And fondling nude statues in parks.

5

A deaf mute who couldn't say "Nay"
Was stuffed by twelve men in one day.
But the Good Lord who guards
Deaf mutes from wild hards
Gave them pox ere their pricks drew away.

6

There was a young fellow named Scott
Who took a girl out on his yacht—
But too lazy to rape her
He made darts of brown paper,
Which he languidly tossed at her twat.

7

"I insist." "It's no good." "But you must."
"Think of me." "Think of masculine lust."
"What a bore." "Why, you whore!
You promised before."
"And the mink! Is that got through trust?"

8

An ancient but jolly old bloke
Once picked up a girl for a poke; First took down her pants,
Fucked her into a trance,
Then shit in her shoe for a joke.

9

There was a young lady named Dowd
Whom a young fellow groped in the crowd.
But the thing that most vexed her
Was that when he stood next her
He said, "How's your cunt?" right out loud.

10

There was a young student of Trinity
Who shattered his sister's virginity.
He buggered his brother,
Had twins by this mother,
And took double honours in Divinity.

11

A mathematician named Hall
Had a hexahedronical ball,
And the cube of its weight
Times his pecker, plus eight,
Was four fifths of five eighths of fuck-all.

12

The gay young Duke of Buckingham
Stood on the bridge at Rockingham
Watching the stunts
Of the cunts and the punts
And the tricks of the pricks that were fucking 'em.

13

There was a young man from Montrose
Who could diddle himself with his toes.
He did it so neat
He fell in love with his feet,
And christened them Myrtle and Rose.

14

The last time I dined with the King
He did quite a curious thing:
He sat on a stool
And took out his tool
And said, "If I play, will you sing?"

15

"Fuck me quick, fuck me deep, fuck me oft
In the bog, in the bath, in the loft,
Up my ass, up my quim,
Knees, armpits, lip rim
With your prick, but *please,* nothing soft."

16

Said Oscar McDingle O'Figgle,
With an almost hysterical giggle,
"Last night I was sick
With delight when my prick
Felt dear Alfred's delicious ass wriggle!"

17

There was a young lady from Brussels
Who was proud of her vaginal muscles.
She could easily plex them
And to interflex them
As to whistle love songs through her bustles.

18

There was a young fellow named Kimble
Whose prick was exceedingly nimble,
But fragile and slender,
And dainty and tender,
So he kept it encased in a thimble.

19

A vice both obscure and unsavory
Kept the Bishop of Chester in slavery:
Midst terrible howls
He deflowered young owls
In his crypt fitted out as an aviary.

20

There was once a sad Maitre d'hotel
Who said, "They can all go to hell!
What they do to my wife—
Why it ruins my life;
And the worst is, they all do it well."

21

A hermit who had an oasis
Thought it the best of all places:
He could pray and be calm
'Neath a pleasant date-palm,
While the lice on his bollocks ran races.

22

There was a young man named Treet
Who minced as he walked down the street.
He wore shoes of bright red,
And playfully said,
I may not be strong, but I'm sweet."

23

There are three ladies of Huxham,
And whenever we meets 'em we fucks 'em.
When that game grows stale
We sits on a rail,
Pulls out our pricks, and they sucks 'em.

24

A preposterous King of Siam
Said, "For women I don't care a damn.
But a fat-bottomed boy
Is my pride and my joy —
They call me a bugger: I am!

25

Then up spake the Bey of Algiers,
"I've been knocking around for long years,
And my language is blunt:
A cunt IS a cunt
And fucking IS fucking"—*(loud cheers)*.

26

Hearing this, mewed the young King of Spain,
To fuck and to bugger is shame.
But it's not infra dig.
To occasionally frig —
So I do it again and again."

27

There was a young fellow named Bliss
Whose sex life was strangely amiss,
For even with Venus
His recalcitrant penis
Would never do better than t
h
i
s

28

A lady while dining at Crewe
Found an elephant's dong in her stew.
Said the waiter, "Don't shout,
And don't wave it about,
Or the others will all want one too."

29

There was a young girl of Darjeeling

Who could dance with such exquisite feeling
There was never a sound
For miles around
Save of fly-buttons hitting the ceiling.

30

When Titian was mixing rose madder,
His model was poised on a ladder.
"Your position," said Titian,
"Inspires coition."
So he nipped up the ladder and 'ad 'er.

31

An organist playing in York
Had a prick that could hold a small fork.
And between obligates
He'd munch at tomatoes,
And keep up his strength while at work.

32

It always delights me at Hanks
To walk up the old river banks.
One time in the grass
I stepped on an ass,
And heard a young girl murmur, "Thanks!"

33

"Far dearer to me than my treasure,"
The heiress declared, "is my leisure.
For then I can screw
The whole Harvard crew—
They're slow, but that lengthens the pleasure."

34

There was a young man from the Coast
Who had an affair with a ghost.
At the height of the orgasm
Said the pallid phantasm,
"I thinly I can feel it —almost!"

35

There was a young lady from Kew
Who filled her vagina with glue.
She said with a grin,
' If they pay to get in,
They'll pay to get out of it too."

36

Here's to it, and through it, and to it again,
To suck it, and screw it, and screw it again!
So in with it, out with it,
Lord work his will with it!
Never a day we don't do it again!

37

There was a debauched little wench
Whom nothing could ever make blench.
She admitted men's poles
At all possible holes,
And she'd 'bugger, fuck, jerk off, and french.

38

A fellow whose surname was Hunt
Trained his cock to perform a slick stunt:
This versatile spout
Could be turned inside out,
Like a glove, and be used as a cunt.

39

There was a young man of St. James
Who indulged in the jolliest games:
He lighted the rim
Of his grandmother's quim,
And laughed as she pissed through the flames.

40

There was a young maid named Clottery
Who was having a fuck on a rockery.
She said, "Listen chum,
You've come on my bum!
This isn't a fuck, it's a mockery."

41

There was a young lady named Hitchin
Who was scratching her crotch in the kitchen.
Her mother said, "Rose,
It's the crabs, I suppose."
She said, "Yes, and the buggers are itchin'."

42

There was a young man of Coblenz
Whose bollocks were simply immense:
It took forty-four draymen,
A priest and three laymen
To carry them thither and thence.

43

There was a young sailor named Bates
Who did the fandango on skates.
He fell on his cutlass
Which rendered him nutless
And practically useless on dates.

44

An agreeable girl named Miss Doves
Likes to jack off the young men she loves.
She will use her bare fist
If the fellows insist
But she really prefers to wear gloves.

45

There was a young man of Canute
Who was troubled by warts on his root.
He put acid on these,
And now, when he pees,
He can finger his root like a flute.

46

A sweet young strip-dancer named Jane
Wore five inches of thin cellophane.
When asked why she wore it
She said, "I abhor it,
But my cunt juice would spatter like rain."

47

The Rajah of Afghanistan
Imported a Birmingham can,
Which he set as a throne
On a great Buddha stone—
But he crapped out-of-doors like a man.

48

A scandal involving an oyster
Sent the Countess of Clewes to a cloister.
She preferred it in bed
To the Count, so she said,
Being longer, and stronger, and moister.

49

There was a young lady of Trent
Who said that she knew what it meant
When he asked her to dine,
Private room, lost of wine,
She knew, oh she knew!—but she went!

50

A lady on climbing Mount Shasta
Complained as the mountain grew vaster,
That it wasn't the climb
Nor the dirt and the grime,
But the ice on her ass that harassed her.

51

A wonderful tribe are the Sweenies,
Renowned for the length of their peenies.
The hair on their balls
Sweeps the floors in their halls,
But they don't look at women —the meanies.

52

When a woman in strapless attire
Found her breasts working higher and higher,
A guest, with great feeling,
Exclaimed, "How appealing!
Do you mind if I piss in the fire?"

53

There was a young Angel called Cary
Who kissed, stroked and fucked Virgin Mary.
And Christ was so bored
At seeing Mom whored
That he set Himself up as a fairy.

54

There was a young girl of Devon
Who was raped in the garden by seven
High Anglican Priests—
The lascivious beasts—
Of such is the kingdom of Heaven.

55

A remarkable race are the Persians,
They have such peculiar diversions.
They screw the whole day
In the regular way,
And save up the nights for perversions.

56

There was a young man of Bengal
Who went to a fancy dress ball.
He was draped like a tree
Having failed to foresee
Being pissed on by dogs, cats, and all.

57

A maiden who lived in Virginny
Had a cunt that could bark, neigh and whinny.
The hunting set chased her,
Fucked, buggered, then dropped her
For the pitch of her organ went tinny.

58

" 'Tis my custom," said dear Lady Norris,
"To beg lifts from the drivers of lorries.
When they get out to piss
I see things that I miss
At the wheel of my two-seater Morris."

59

There was a young lady, named Ransom
Who was futtered three times in a hansom.
When she called for more
A voice from the floor
Said, "My name is Simpson, not Samson.

60

A mediaeval recluse named Sissions
Was alarmed by his nightly emissions.
His cell-mate, a sod,
Said, "Leave it to God."
And taught him some nifty positions..

61

In the city of Paris are wives
Who, when not scratching their hives,
Are waiting for tourists
Who might act as purists
And give them the ride of their lives.

62

There was a young artist named Frentzel
Whose tool was as sharp as a pencil.
He pricked through an actress,
The sheet and the mattress,
And busted the bedroom utensil.

63

All the lady-apes ran from King Kong
For his dong was unspeakably long.
But a friendly giraffe
Quaffed his yard and a half,
And ecstatically burst into song.

64

The prior of Dunstan St. Just,
Consumed with erotical lust,
Raped the bishop's prize jowls,
Buggered four startled owls
And a little green lizard, that bust.

65

"In my salad days," said Lady Bierley
"I took my cocks fairly and squarely.
But now when they come

They go right up my bum—
And that only happens but rarely."

66

The Marquesa de Excusador
Used to pee on the drawing-room floor,
For the can was so cold
And when one grows old
To be much alone is a bore.

67

"It's been a very full day,"
Yawned Lady Mary McDougle McKay.
"Three cherry tarts,
At least twenty farts,
Two shits and a bloody fine lay."

68

An elderly pervert in Nice
Who was long past wanting a piece
Would jack-off his hogs,
His cows and his dogs,
Till his parrot called in the police.

69

"Great God!" wailed Peter McGuff,
"What the devil is all of this stuff!
She twiddles my prick,
Gets it stiff as a stick,
And denies me the use of her muff."

70

There was a young parson named Binns
Who talked about women and things.
But his secret desire
Was a boy in the choir
With a bottom like jelly on springs.

71

There was a young Scot of Delray
Who buggered his father one day,
Saying, "I like it rather
To stuff it up Father;
He's clean—and there's nothing to pay."

72

There was an old man of Dundee,
Who came home as drunk as could be.
He wound up the clock
With the end of his cock,
And buggared his wife with the key.

73

There was a young plumber of Lea
Who was plumbing a girl by the sea.
She said, "Stop your plumbing;
There's somebody coming!"
Said the plumber, still plumbing, "It's me."

74

There was a young nun from Siberia
Endowed with a virgin interior —
Until an old monk
Jumped into her bunk,
And now she's the Mother Superior.

75

There was an old critic named West
Whose penis came up to his chest.
He said, 'I declare,
I have no pubic hair."
So he covered his nuts with his vest.

76

The nephew of one of the czars
Used to suck off Rasputin at Yars,
'Til the peasants revolted,
The royal family bolted—
Now they're under the sickle and stars.

77

There was a young man of Belgravia,
Who cared neither for God nor his Saviour.
He walked down the Strand
With his balls in his hand,
And was had up for indecent behaviour.

78

There was a young lady named Alice
Who was having a piss in a chalice.
What a stunt," said a monk,
To twiddle your cunt,
Not through need but through Protestant malice."

79

A young man with passions quite gingery
Tore a hole in his sister's best lingerie.
He slapped her behind
And made up his mind
To add incest to insult and injury.

80

There was a young German named Ringer
Who was screwing an opera singer.
Said he with a grin,
"Well, I've sure got it in!"
Said she, "You mean that ain't your finger?"

82

That naughty old Sappho of Greece
Said, "What I prefer to a piece
Is to have my pudenda
Rubbed hard by the enda
The little pink nose of my niece."

82

A class-mate of William Dean Howells
Shot his sperm o'er a young coed's bowels.
He said, "I regret
That I've made you so wet —
And I fear I am quite out of towels."

83

There was a young maiden named Rose,
With erogenous zones in her toes.
She remained onanistic
'Til a foot-fetichistic
Young man became one of her beaux.

84

There was an old man who could piss
Through a ring—and what's more, never miss.
Marksmen queued up to cheer,
Bought him beer after beer,
And swore oaths on his urinal hiss.

85

There was a young man of high station
Who was found by a pious relation
Making love in a ditch
To—*I won't say a bitch*—
But a woman of no reputation.

86

A broken-down harlot named Tupps
Was heard to confess in her cups:
"The height of my folly
Was fucking a collie—
But I got a nice price for the pups."

87

A passionate red-headed girl,
When you kissed her, her senses would whirl,
And her twat would get wet
And would wiggle and fret,
And her cunt-lips would curl and unfurl.

88

There was a young man from Lynn
Whose cock was the size of a pin.
Said his girl with a laugh
As she fondled his staff,
"This won't be much of a sin."

89

There was an old Count of Swoboda
Who would not pay a whore what he owed her.
So with great *savoir-faire*
She stood on a chair,
And pissed in his whiskey-and-soda.

90

To his bride a young bridegroom said,
"Pish! your cunt is as big as a dish!"
She replied, "Why, you fool,
With your limp little tool
It's like driving a nail with a fish!"

91

There was a young fellow named Brewster
Who said to his wife as he goosed her,
"It used to be grand
But just look at my hand!
You ain't wiping as clean as you used to,"

92

There was a young lady of Twickenham,
Who regretted that men had no prick in 'em.
On her knees every day,
To her God she would pray
To lengthen, and strengthen, and thicken 'em.

93

A base-drummer out in Madras
Had bollocks made out of brass.
In wintery weather

They rattled together
And spares came out of his ass.

94

There was a young girl named McCall
Whose cunt was exceedingly small,
But the size of her anus
Was something quite heinous—
It could hold seven pricks and one ball.

95

A cretin who lived in an attic
Was fallaciously rated as static;
But how little they knew—
His knob was not blue—
But hoary and necrophilatic.

96

There was a young girl of Dundee
Who was raped by an ape in a tree.
The result was most horrid —
All ass and no forehead,
Three balls and a purple goatee.

97

There was a young man from Cape Cod
Who put his own mother in pod.
His name? It was Tucker,
The Bugger, The Fucker,
The Bleeder, The Bastard, The Sod.

98

Thus spake I AM THAT I AM:
For the Virgin I don't give a damn,
What pleases me most
Is to buggar the Ghost,
And then be sucked off by the Lamb.

99

There was a young man of Nantucket,
Whose prick was so long he could suck it.
He said, with a grin,
As he wiped off his chin,
"If my ear was a cunt I could fuck it"

100

When a lecherous curate at Leeds
Was discovered, one day, in the weeds
Astride a young nun,
He said, "Christ, this is fun!
Far better than telling one's beads!"

101

There was a young lady of Crewe
Whose cherry a chap had got through
Which she told to her mother
Who fixed her another
Out of rubber and red ink and glue.

102

A worried young man from Stamboul
Discovered red spots on his tool.
Said the doctor, a cynic,
"Get out of my clinic!
Just wipe off the lipstick, you fool."

103

There was a young dancer, Priscilla,
Who flavored her cunt with vanilla.
The taste was so fine,
Men and beasts stood in line,
Including a stud armadilla.

104

The priest, a cocksucker named Sheen,
Is delighted his sins are not seen.
"Though God sees through walls,"
Says Monsignor, "—Oh, balls!
This God stuff is simply a screen.

105

There was a young girl in Alsace
Who was having her first piece of ass.
"Oh, darling you'll kill me!
Oh, dearest, you thrill me
Like Father John's thumb after mass!

106

There was a young maid from Mobile
Whose cunt was made of blue steel!
She got her thrills
From pneumatic drills,
And off-centered emery wheels.

107

There was a young hermit named Dave,
Who kept a dead whore in his cave.
He said, "I'll admit,
I'm a bit of a shit,
But think of the money I save."

108

A modern young lady named Hall
Went out to a birth-control ball.
She was loaded with pessaries
And other accessories,
But no one approached her at all.

109

There was an old man of Duluth
Whose cock was shot off in his youth.
He fucked with his nose
And with fingers and toes,
And he came through a hole in his tooth.

110

A handsome young monk in a wood
Told a girl she should cling to the good.
She obeyed him, and gladly;
He repulsed her, but sadly:
"My dear, you have misunderstood."

111

There was a young girl from Sofia
Who succumbed to her lover's desire.
She said, "It's a sin,
But now that it's in,
Could you shove it a few inches higher?"

112

A young bride was once heard to say,
"Oh dear, I am wearing away!
The insides of my thighs
Look just like mince pies,
For my husband won't shave every day.

113

There was a young man of St. Johns
Who wanted to bugger the swans.
"Oh no," said the porter,
"You bugger my daughter,
Them swans is reserved for the Dons."

114

There was a young man from Axminster
Whose designs were quite base and quite sinister
His lifelong ambition
Was anal coition
With the wife of the French foreign minister.

115

There was a young lady of Louth,
Who returned from a trip to the South.
Her papa said "Nelly,
There's more in your belly,
Than ever went in by your mouth."

116

A team playing baseball in Dallas
Called the umpire a shit out of malice.
While this worthy had fits,
The team made eight hits
And a girl in the bleachers named Alice.

117

In the Garden of Eden lay Adam,
Complacently stroking his madam,
And loud was his mirth
For on all of the earth
There were only two balls —and he had 'em.

118

"For the tenth time, dull Daphnis," said Chloe,
"You have told me my bosom is snowy;
You have made much fine verse on
Each part of my person,
Now *do* something—there's a good boy!"

119

There was a young girl of Detroit
Who at fucking was very adroit:
She could squeeze her vagina
To a pin-point, or finer,
Or open it out like a quoit.

120

And she had a friend named Durand
Whose cock could contract or expand.
He could diddle a midge
Or the arch of a bridge —
Their performance together was grand!

121

There was a young lady named Hall
Wore a newspaper dress to a ball.
The dress caught on fire
And burned her entire
Front page, sporting section, and all.

122

A disgusting young man named McGill
Made his neighbors exceedingly ill
When they learned of his habits
Involving white rabbits
And a bird with a flexible bill.

123

There was a young sailor from Brighton
Who remarked to his girl, "You're a tight one."
She replied, "'Pon my soul,
You're in the wrong hole;
There's plenty of room in the right one.

124

There was a young fellow from Leeds
Who swallowed a package of seeds.
Great tufts of grass
Sprouted out of his ass
And his balls were all covered with weeds.

125

There was a young girl whose divinity
Preserved her in perfect virginity,
Till a candle, her nemesis,
Caused parthenogenesis —
Now she thinks herself one of the Trinity.

126

In the reign of King George the third,
The fashionable fuck was a bird:
The hole of a sparrow
Was dry, pink and narrow,
And was oiled with hummingbirds' turd.

127

The nipples of Sarah Sarong,
When excited, are twelve inches long.
This embarrassed her lover
Who was pained to discover
She expected no less of his dong.

128

There was a young lady named Nelly
Whose tits could be joggled like jelly.
They could tickle her twat,
Or be tied in a foot,
And could even swat flies on her belly.

129

"The testes are cooler outside,"
Said the doc to the curious bride.
"For the semen must not
Get too fucking hot,
And the bag fans your bum on the ride."

130

There was a young lady named Gloria
Who was had by Sir Gerald Du Maurier,
And then by six men,
Sir Gerald again,
And the band at the Waldorf-Astoria.

131

Said Edna St Vincent Millay
As she lay in the hay all asplay,
"If you can make wine
From these grapes, I opine,
We'll stay in this barn until May."

132

There was an old parson of Lundy,
Fell asleep in his vestry on Sunday.
He awoke with a scream:
"What, another wet dream!
That's what comes from not frigging since Monday."

133

A chap down in Oklahoma
Had a cock that could sing La Paloma,
But the sweetness of pitch
Couldn't put off the hitch
Of impotence, size and aroma.

134

The grand-niece of Madame Du Barry
Suspected her son was a fairy.
"It's peculiar," said she,
"But he sits down to pee,
And stands when I bathe the canary."

135

A gentleman living in Fife
Made love to the corpse of his wife.
"How could I know, Judge?
She was cold, did not budge—
Just the same as she'd acted in life."

136

While pissing on deck, an old boatswain
Fell asleep, and his pisser got frozen.
It snapped at the shank
It fell off and sank
In the sea — 'twas his own fault for dozin'!

137

When a girl, young Elizabeth Barrett
Was found by her Ma in a garret,
She had shoved up a diamond
As far as her hymen,
And was ramming it home with a carrot.

138

There was a young fellow of Mayence
Who fucked his own ass in defiance
Not only of habit
And morals but —damn it!—
Most of the known laws of science.

139

There was a young lady of Cheam
Who crept into the vestry unseen.
She pulled down her knickers,
Likewise the vicar's
And said, "How about it, old bean?"

140

"At a seance," said a young man named Post,
"I was being sucked off by a ghost;
Someone switched on the lights
And there in gauze tights,
On his knees, was Tobias mine host."

141

*There was a young man of Dunfries
Who said to his girl, "If you please,
It would give me great bliss
If, while playing with this,
You would pay some attention to these!"*

142

There was a gay Countess of Bray,
And you may think it odd when I say,
That in spite of high station,
Rank and education,
She always spelt Cunt with a K.

143

In his garden remarked Lord Larkeeling:
"A fig for your digging and weeding.
I like watching birds
While they're dropping their turds,
And spying on guinea pigs breeding."

144

*There was a young couple named Kelly
Who were found stuck belly to belly,
Because in their haste,
They used library paste,
Instead of petroleum jelly.*

145

There once was a girl named Louise
Whose cunt-hair hung down to her knees.
The crabs in her twat
Tied the hair in a knot,
And constructed a flying trapeze.

146

An ignorant maiden named Rewlid
Did something amazingly stupid:
When her lover had spent
She douched with cement,
And gave birth to a statue of Cupid.

147

There was a young girl of Kilkenny
On whose genital parts there were many
Venereal growths —
The result of wild oats
Sown there by a fellow named Benny.

148

The modern cinematic emporium
Is not just a super-sensorium
But a highly effectual
Heterosexual
Mutual masturbatorium.

149

When Brother John wanted a screw
He would stuff a fat cat in a shoe,
Pull up his cassock
And kneel on a hassock
While doing his damnedest to mew.

150

A psychoneurotic fanatic
Said, "I take little girls to the attic,
Then whistle a tune
'Bout the cow and the moon—
When the cow jumps, I come. It's dramatic!

156

The jolly old Bishop of Birmingham
He buggered three maids while confirming 'em.
As they knelt seeking God
He excited his rod
And pumped his episcopal sperm in 'em.

152

There once was a horny old bitch
With a motorized self-fucker which
She would use with delight
All day long and all night —
Twenty bucks: Abercrombie and Fitch.

153

"It's dull in Duluth, Minnesota,
Of spirit there's not an iota—"
Complained Alice to Joe
Who tried not to show
That he yawned in her snatch as he blowed her.

154

The Shah of the Empire of Persia
Lay for days in a sexual merger.
When the nautch asked the Shah,
Won't you ever withdraw?"
He replied with a yawn, "It's inertia"

155

When aged, the playwright Racine —
Who was weaned at the age of sixteen—
Remarked, "I'll admit
'Twas a slack, milkless tit,
But think of the fun it had been."

156

There was a young curate of Eltham
Who wouldn't fuck girls, but he felt 'em.
In lanes he would linger
And play at stick-finger,
And scream with delight when he smelt 'em.

157

A disciple of symbolist Jung,
Asked his wife, "May I bugger your bung?"
And was so much annoyed
When he found she read Freud,
He went out in the yard and ate dung.

158

There once was a Monarch of Spain
Who was terribly haughty and vain.
When women were nigh
He'd unbutton his fly,
And screw them with signs of disdain.

159

Said the Duchess of Danzer at tea,
"Young man, do you fart when you pee?"
I replied with some wit,
"Do you belch when you shit?"
I think that was one up for me.

160

A marine being sent to Hong Kong
Got a doctor to alter his dong.
He sailed off with a tool
Flat and thin as a rule —
When he got there he found he was wrong.

161

A finicky young whippersnapper
Had ways so revoltingly dapper
That a young lady's quim
Didn't interest him
If it hadn't a cellophane wrapper.

162

"Well, I took your advice" said McKnopp,
"And told the wife to get up on top.
She bounced about a bit,
Didn't quite get the hang of it,
"And the kids, much amused, made us stop."

163

There was a young fellow named Sweeney
Whose girl was a terrible meanie.
The hatch of her snatch
Had a catch that would latch —
She could only be screwed by Houdini.

164

There once was a harlot named Gail
Whose price was tattooed on her tail;
And on her behind,
For the sake of the blind,
She there had it written in Braille.

165

There was a young lady of Rheims
Who amazingly pissed four streams.
A friend poked around
And a fly-button found
Wedged tightly in one of her seams.

166

A geneticist living in Delft,
Scientifically played with himself;
When he was done
He labeled it: *Son,*
And filed him away on a shelf.

167

While fucking one night, Dr. Zuck
In his ears got his wife's nipples stuck.
With his thumb up her bum,
He could hear himself come—
Thus inventing the Telephone Fuck.

168

There was a young lady of Wheeling
Who professed to lack sexual feeling.
But a cynic named Boris
Just touched her clitoris,
And she had to be scraped off the ceiling.

169

There was a young fellow named Howell
Who buggered himself with a trowel.
The triangular shape
Was conducive to rape,
And was easily cleaned with a towel.

170

There was a young man from Port Said
Who fell down a shit-house and died.
His unfortunate mother,
She jell down another;
And now they're interred side by side.

171

A gentle old Dame they called Muir
Had a mind so delightfully pure
That she fainted away
At a friend's house one day
When she saw some canary manure.

172

There was an old whore named McGee
Who was just the right sort for a spree.
She said, "For a fuck
I charge half a buck,
And I throw in the ass-hole for free."

173

I dined with Lord Hughy Fitz-Bluing
Who said, "Do you squirm when you're screwing?"
I replied "Simple shagging
Without any wagging
Is only for screwing canoeing."

174

There was a young man in Woods Hole
Who had an affair with a mole.
Though a bit of a nancy
He *did* like to fancy
Himself in the dominant role.

175

There was a young lady named Hilda
Who went for a walk with a builder.
He knew that he could,
And he should, and he would—
And he did—and he goddam' near killed her!!

176

Remind me, dear, said Sir Keith,
"As soon us I've brushed my teeth,
To tale down this glass
And examine my ass
From behind —and of course from beneath?

177

A pious young lady named Finnegan
Would caution her friend, "Well, you're in again;
So time it aright,
Make it last through the night,
For I certainly don't want to sin again!"

178

A circus performer named Ditti
Was subject to passionate fits,
But his pleasure in life
Was to suck off his wife
As he swung by his knees from her tits.

179

Young girls who frequent picture-palaces
Are amused at the vogue of analysis,
And giggle that Freud
Should be less than annoyed
While they tickle contemporary phalluses.

180

A musical student from Sparta
Was a truly magnificent farter:
On the strength of one bean
He'd fart God Save the Queen,
And Beethoven's Moonlight Sonata.

181

An avant-garde bard named McNamiter
Had a tool of enormous diameter.
But it wasn't the size

Brought tears to her eyes.
'Tivas the rhythm —dactylic hexameter!

182

There was a young girl of Peru
Who had nothing whatever to do,
So she sat on the stairs
And counted cunt hairs—
Four thousand, three hundred, and two.

183

There was a young fellow of Eversham
Wrote a treatise on cunts and on sucking them.
But a lady from Wales
Took the wind from his sails
With an essay on ass-holes and fucking them.

184

"Now listen, young girl," said McPhett,
"You tell me your cunt is all wet.
Yet when I shove, you squirm,
Waste my boiling hot sperm —
You don't want to fuck, only sweat!"

185

A milkmaid there was, with a stutter,
Who was lonely and wanted a futter.
She had nowhere to turn,
So she straddled a churn,
And managed to come with the butter.

186

Dr. John Donne, a Dean to St. Paul
Grew old, and his prick rather small.
Though he buggered a bug
At the edge of a rug,
The insect scarce felt it at all.

187

There once was a sailor from Wales,
An expert at pissing in gales,
He could piss in a jar
From the top-gallant spar
Without even wetting the sails.

188

A wage-conscious floozie named Annie
Had prices both cosy and canny:
A buck for a fuck,
Fifty cents for a suck,
And a dime for a feel of her fanny.

189

*In the speech of his time, did the Bard
Refer to his prick as his "yard,"
But sigh no more, madams
'Twas no longer than Adam's
Or mine, and not one half so hard.*

190

Cleopatra, while helping to pump,
Ground out such a furious bump
That Antony's dick
Snapped off like a stick,
And left him to pump with the stump

191

There once was a curate named Swope
Who wanted to bugger the Pope—
To destroy the division
Twixt his lust and religion
And, on the side, get an Archbishop's cope.

192

*There was a young lady of Natchez
Who chanced to be born with two snatches,
And she often said, "Shit!
Why, I'd give either tit
For a man with equipment that matches"*

193

There was a young fellow named Lock
Who was born with a two-headed cock.
When he'd fondle the thing
It would rise up and sing
An antiphonal chorus by Bach.

194

But whether these two ever met
Has not been recorded as yet —
Still, it would be diverting
To see him inserting
His whang while it sang a duet!

195

There was a young girl of East Lynne
Whose mother, to save her from sin,
Had filled up her crack
With hard-setting shellac —
But the boys picked it out with a pin.

196

King Louis gave lessons in Class.
One time he was sexing a lass,
When she used the word "Damn"
He rebuked her: "Please ma'am,
Keep a more civil tongue in my ass."

197

In spite of a wasting disease
O'Reilly went down on his knees
Before altars of gods,
Whores, boys, and small clogs —
And all this for very small fees.

198

A piano composer named Liszt
Played with one hand while he pissed.
But as he grew older
His technique grew bolder,
And in concert jacked off with his fist.

199

There lives a young girl in New York
Who is cautious from fear of the stork.
You will find she is taped
To prevent being raped,
And her ass-hole is plugged with a cork.

200

In bed Dr. Oscar McPugh
Spoke of Spengler —and ate crackers too.
His wife said, Oh, stuff
That philosophy guff
Up your ass, dear, and throw me a screw!'

201

A Sunday-School student in Mass.
Soon rose to the head of the class,
By reciting quite bright
And by sleeping at night
With his tongue up the minister's ass.

202

While out on a picnic, McFee
Was stung on the balls by a bee.
He made oodles of money
By oozing pure honey
Every time he attempted to pee.

203

There was a young lady named Wylde,
Who kept herself quite undefiled
By thinking of Jesus,
Contagious diseases,
And the bother of having a child.

204

There was a young man of Bombay
Who fashioned a cunt out of clay.
The heat of his prick
Turned the damn thing to brick,
And wore all his foreskin away.

205

To succeed in the brothels at Derna
One always begins as a learner.
Indentured at six
As a greaser of prices,
One may rise to be fitter and turner.

206

There was a young lady whose joys
Were achieved with incomparable poise.
She could have an orgasm
With never a spasm—
She could fart without making a noise.

207

When Theocritus guarded his flock
He piped in the shade of a rock.
It is said that his Muse
Was one of the ewes
With a bum life a pink hollyhock.
THE END

Index of First Lines

'Twas at the gatherin' of the Clans, ... 39

'Twas on the good ship Venus, ... 36

"'Tis my custom," said dear Lady Norris,... 109

"At a seance," said a young man named Post,........................ 129

"Far dearer to me than my treasure,".......... 103

"For the tenth time, dull Daphnis," said Chloe, ... 124

"Fuck me quick, fuck me deep, fuck me oft..... 98

"Great God!" wailed Peter McGuff,......... 112

"I insist." "It's no good." "But you must." 96

"In my salad days," said Lady Bierley 111

"It's been a very full day," 111

"It's dull in Duluth, Minnesota,............. 133

"Now listen, young girl," said McPhett, ... 141

"The testes are cooler outside," 127

"Well, I took your advice" said McKnopp,............... 135

A base-drummer out in Madras 118

A broken-down harlot named Tupps.......... 116

A chap down in Oklahoma 128

A circus performer named Ditti 140

A class-mate of William Dean Howells........ 115

A cretin who lived in an attic........................ 118

A deaf mute who couldn't say "Nay" 96

150

A disciple of symbolist Jung, ... 134

A disgusting young man named McGill 125

A farmer's dog once came to town 63

A fellow whose surname was Hunt 104

A finicky young whippersnapper 135

A geneticist living in Delft, ... 137

A gentle old Dame they called Muir 138

A gentleman living in Fife 128

A handsome young monk in a wood 122

A hermit who had an oasis 100

A lady on climbing Mount Shasta 107

A lady while dining at Crewe 101

A maiden who lived in Virginny 109

A marine being sent to Hong Kong 134

A mathematician named Hall 97

A mediaeval recluse named Sissions 109

A milkmaid there was, with a stutter, ... 142

A miner coming home one night 47

A modern young lady named Hall 121

A musical student from Sparta 140

A passionate red-headed girl, ... 116

A piano composer named Liszt 145

A pious young lady named Finnegan 140

A preposterous King of Siam 100

A psychoneurotic fanatic 132

A remarkable race are the Persians, ... 108

151

A sailor told me 'ere he died,........................... 7

A scandal involving an oyster...................... 106

A Sunday-School student in Mass................... 146

A sweet young strip-dancer named Jane 106

A team playing baseball in Dallas................. 123

A vice both obscure and unsavory.................. 99

A wage-conscious floozie named Annie.......... 142

A wonderful tribe are the Sweenies,................ 107

A worried young man from Stamboul 120

A young bride was once heard to say,........... 122

A young man with passions quite gingery 114

All the lady-apes ran from King Kong.... 110

All the nice girls love a candle,..................... 83

An agreeable girl named Miss Doves 105

An Alderman, a wealthy cit, ... 56

An ancient but jolly old bloke......................... 96

An avant-garde bard named McNamiter. 141

An elderly pervert in Nice 111

An ignorant maiden named Rewlid........ 131

An organist playing in York 102

And she had a friend named Durand 124

Arseholes are cheap today,........................ 68

As she walked along the Bois de Boulogne.... 43

At the call of the last trumpet, ... 59

Brisk Friar John, a merry weight,..................... 54

152

But whether these two ever met 144

Cats on the rooftops, ... 70

Caviare comes from the virgin sturgeon. 44

Cleopatra, while helping to pump, ... 143

Come away my love with me 34

Come prick up your ears, and attend Sirs, awhile; 37

Dr. John Donne, a Dean to St. Paul 142

Hear us sing of Sergeant Boon, ... 25

Hearing this, mewed the young King of Spain, ... 101

Here's to it, and through it, and to it again, .. 103

I dined with Lord Hughy Fitz-Bluing 139

I don't want to join the army, ... 62

I dreamed my love lay in her bed: 65

I left the party early, just after half-past nine, . 75

I'll tell you a ditty that's certain to please, ... 80

I've just come away from a wedding, ... 51

If Leo your own birthday marks 95

In bed Dr. Oscar McPugh 145

In days of yore there lived a whore, ... 72

In his garden remarked Lord Larkeeling: ... 130

In spite of a wasting disease 145

In the city of Paris are wives 110

In the Garden of Eden lay Adam, ... 124

In the Harems of Egypt, close-guarded and secret, ... 86

In the reign of King George the third, ... 126

153

In the shade of the old apple tree, ... 20

In the speech of his time, did the Bard 143

In the street of A Thousand Arseholes, 61

It always delights me at Hanks 102

King Louis gave lessons in Class................... 144

Last night, ... 52

Life presents a doleful picture, ... 34

Little Sally based her hopes 63

My ambition's to go on the stage; 15

Now here's a pretty little song so listen if you will 49

Now, down our street we had a crashing party, 84

Oh gather round lovers and listen to me; 82

Oh the shitehawks they fly high in Mobile, .. 20

Ollie, Ollie, Ollie, ... 68

Once I was a servant girl who worked in Drury Lane, ... 42

Please don't burn our shithouse down, ... 78

Recent extensive researches................. 16

Remind me, dear, said Sir Keith, ... 139

Rosalind, a pretty young lass, ... 95

Said Edna St Vincent Millay 127

Said Oscar McDingle O'Figgle, ... 98

Said the Duchess of Danzer at tea, ... 134

She lay nude between the sheets....................... 35

She was poor but she was honest 12

She was sweet sixteen, Little Angeline, ... 18

She went for a drive in a Morgan, ... 58

154

Sitting in O'Riley's bar one day 87

Some girls work in fact'ries some girls work in stores, ... 88

Tell me, friend John—do, if you can, ... 55

That naughty old Sappho of Greece 115

The Bey of Algiers when afraid for his ears, ... 8

The gay young Duke of Buckingham 97

The grand-niece of Madame Du Barry. 128

The jolly old Bishop of Birmingham 132

The Lady of the Manor, ... 78

The last time I dined with the King 98

The Marquesa de Excusado 111

The minstrels sing of a bastard King 21

The modern cinematic emporium 131

The nephew of one of the czars 113

The nipples of Sarah Sarong, ... 126

The portions of a woman that appeal to man's depravity, ... 14

The priest, a cocksucker named Sheen, ... 120

The prior of Dunstan St. Just, ... 110

The Rajah of Afghanistan 106

The Shah of the Empire of Persia 133

The sun shone on the village green, ... 60

The team of Tom and Louise 95

Then up spake the Bey of Algiers, ... 101

There are three ladies of Huxham, ... 100

There lives a young girl in New York 145

155

There once was a curate named Swope 143

There once was a girl named Louise 131

There once was a harlot named Gail 135

There once was a horny old bitch 132

There once was a Monarch of Spain .. 134

There was a debauched little wench 104

There was a gay Countess of Bray, ... 130

There was a priest a dirty beast, ... 83

There was a puritanical lad 38

There was a Rajah of Astrakan, Yo Ho! 69

There was a ram of Derbyshire 43

There was a young Angel called Cary 108

There was a young artist named Frentzel 110

There was a young couple named Kelly 130

There was a young curate of Eltham 133

There was a young dancer, Priscilla, ... 120

There was a young fellow from Leeds 125

There was a young fellow named Bliss 101

There was a young fellow named Brewster 117

There was a young fellow named Howell 138

There was a young fellow named Kimble 99

There was a young fellow named Lock 144

There was a young fellow named Scott 96

There was a young fellow named Sweeney 135

There was a young fellow of Eversham 141

There was a young fellow of Mayence 129

*There was a young
German named Ringer* 114

There was a young girl
from Sofia 122

There was a young girl in
Alsace 121

There was a young girl
named McCall 118

*There was a young girl of
Darjeeling* 102

There was a young girl of
Detroit 124

There was a young girl of
Devon 108

*There was a young girl of
Dundee* 118

*There was a young girl of
East Lynne* 144

*There was a young girl of
Kilkenny* 131

There was a young girl of
Peru 141

*There was a young girl
whose divinity* 126

There was a young hermit
named Dave, ... 121

There was a young lady
from Brussels 99

*There was a young lady
from Kew* 103

There was a young lady
named Alice 114

There was a young lady
named Dowd 97

*There was a young lady
named Gloria* 127

There was a young lady
named Hall 125

There was a young lady
named Hilda 139

There was a young lady
named Hitchin 105

*There was a young lady
named Nelly* 126

*There was a young lady
named Wylde,* 146

*There was a young lady
of Cheam* 129

*There was a young lady
of Crewe* 120

There was a young lady
of Exeter, ... 95

There was a young lady
of Louth, ... 123

There was a young lady
of Natchez 143

There was a young lady
of Rheims 137

There was a young lady
of Trent.................. 107

There was a young lady
of Twickenham, ... 117

There was a young lady
of Wheeling 137

There was a young lady
whose joys............. 147

There was a young lady,
named Ransom 109

There was a young maid
from Mobile........... 121

There was a young maid
named Clottery....... 104

There was a young
maiden named Rose,
.... 115

There was a young man
from Axminster 123

There was a young man
from Cape Cod 119

There was a young man
from Lynn 116

There was a young man
from Montrose 98

There was a young man
from Port Said 138

There was a young man
from the Coast 103

There was a young man
in Woods Hole 139

There was a young man
named Treet 100

There was a young man
of Belgravia, ... 114

There was a young man
of Bengal 108

There was a young man
of Bombay............. 146

There was a young man
of Canute 106

There was a young man
of Coblenz............. 105

158

There was a young man of Dunfries 130

There was a young man of high station 116

There was a young man of Nantucket, ... 119

There was a young man of St. James 104

There was a young man of St. Johns 123

There was a young nun from Siberia 113

There was a young parson named Binns.......... 112

There was a young plumber of Lea 113

There was a young sailor from Brighton 125

There was a young sailor named Bates 105

There was a young Scot of Delray 112

There was a young student of Trinity 97

There was an old Count of Swoboda 117

There was an old critic named West 113

There was an old lady who lived down our street,....................... 46

There was an old man of Duluth 122

There was an old man of Dundee, ... 112

There was an old man who could piss 115

There was an old parson of Lundy,.............. 127

There was an old sailor who sat on a rock 17

There was an old whore named McGee 138

There was once a sad Maitre d'hotel 99

There's a man that sits in prison 75

They're diggin' up Father's grave to build a sewer: 89

This is the tale of Dead-Eye Dick,................ 84

159

This is the tale of Sonia
    Snell 48

Three old whores from
    Winnipeg 53

Thus spake I AM THAT I
    AM: 119

To his bride a young
    bridegroom said, ... 117

To succeed in the brothels
    at Derna 147

Walking in a meadow
    green, ... 23

Way down in Alberta .. 66

When a girl, young
    Elizabeth Barrett ... 129

When a lecherous curate
    at Leeds 119

When a man grows old
    and his balls grow cold
    an the 26

When a woman in
    strapless attire 107

When aged, the
    playwright Racine —
    133

When Brother John
    wanted a screw 132

When I got home on
    Saturday night as
    drunk as a cunt 76

When the bricklayer's
    union struck, ... 85

When Theocritus guarded
    his flock 147

When Titian was mixing
    rose madder, ... 102

While fucking one night,
    Dr. Zuck 137

While out on a picnic,
    McFee 146

While pissing on deck, an
    old boatswain 128

Young girls who frequent
    picture-palaces 140

Printed in the United States
211756BV00002B/38/A